Ohferdumb
Growing Up
on a farm in
Minnesota

The Early Years

By
Mike Cournia

DEDICATION

Dedicated to my mom, my siblings, my loving wife, and our wonderful daughters and their families. These stories will help the Granddaughters understand why Grandpa is the way he is.

Ohferdumb is a compilation of stories and pictures about growing up in a large family on a farm in northern Minnesota. "Ohferdumb" is a term that our mother affectionately used when one of the seven kids did something dumb, which was not uncommon. Our father died at the young age of 40 from an unexpected heart attack. My mom, at age 36, had to take over the day-to-day running of the farm while raising three girls and four boys. Growing up in a rural community, one had to create their own fun and often there were significant risks involved. These stories and pictures will help the reader get an inside look at what life was like in a small rural farming community in the 50s and 60s.

TABLE OF CONTENTS

CHAPTER 1
WHO RULES THE ROOST

This is the farm that I grew up on in northern Minnesota. It was a wonderful experience. With three brothers and three sisters there was never a dull moment. Today, I have two stories that happened when I was four years old. One I remember like it happened yesterday and the other I do not remember but my mom would often tell the story to us. The white dashes on the picture go with the first story. As you drive down the driveway the first building on the left is the granary, that also housed a chicken coop. The next building is the barn with a silo. The next building coming towards the house was the garage. At the back side of the garage, facing the house, was a big sandbox. We spent countless hours playing in the sandbox. Fortunately, we did not have any cats on the farm. The first story starts in the sandbox.

One day I was playing in the sandbox. My mom was upstairs in the house and peered out the window to check on me. At that time, we had a very nasty rooster. He was overly aggressive. Mom saw the rooster sneaking along the side of the garage heading toward the sandbox. She knew the rooster was coming for me. I remember playing in the sandbox with my back toward the approaching rooster. Before I knew it, this big rooster was on my shoulders flapping its wings and pecking at my head. I remember wondering what was going on. All at once I saw this broom come out of nowhere swinging at the level right above my haircut. Mom to the rescue! She knocked that rooster off, and the rooster took off running. The white dashes show its path. My Uncle Sonny was working in the granary with our hired man, Leo. Uncle Sonny came walking out of the granary to see what all the commotion was. As the rooster was running past him, my mom yelled to Uncle Sonny, "Get that rooster!"

Uncle Sonny chased the rooster out into the barley field behind the granary. They did not get far when the rooster turned on my uncle. Uncle Sonny tried stopping but slipped on the damp ground and was flat on his back. The rooster marched right up Uncle Sonny's body to his head and started to flap its wings on the sides of Uncle Sonny's head. He finally got the rooster off and started running back towards the yard, with the rooster in pursuit. I remember thinking how funny Uncle Sonny was running. It reminded me of the cartoons I had seen where the legs of the person running were running in front of the body. Uncle Sonny ran around the corner of the granary heading towards the barn. Leo, our hired man, stepped out of the granary just in time to see my uncle go by. He also reached down and grabbed the rooster by the neck and did it in! We had chicken stew for dinner that night. It is remarkable how some memories can be so vivid.

The second story, which I do not remember happening, did in fact happen when I was about the same age. Mom had come out of the house looking for my little brother John and me. She called out for us, and she heard us call back. She could not believe her eyes when she saw that my brother John and I had climbed up 40 or 50 feet of a 70-foot silo. The blue marks on the picture show you where we were. There were galvanized steel round bars that circled the silo every 3 feet or so. There was also a second set of bars about 6 inches above each bar. "It was like a big, odd-shaped ladder going all around the silo." Mom said she almost fainted. But she did not. She came over and talked us down off the silo. My brother John was the age of my 2 1/2-year-old granddaughter! It is amazing one of us did not fall. God had other plans for us.

White hair is dominant on both sides of my family. My dad had white hair at an early age as did my mom's dad. Mom always dyed her hair. In later years when the family would get together and retell many stories of life on the farm, we would always comment, "Mom, with all these crazy things happening, you never got one gray hair!" She would always lead the laughter from that comment.

CHAPTER 2
OUR SCARY BARN

The barn and silo on our farm were wonderful places to play. Many cousins called it "the scary barn." The year I was born, Dad and Mom decided to focus more on the land and minimize the farm animals. The hayloft was a fun, but sometimes scary, place to be. It was an open expanse. There was a big rope going up to a pulley system that would lower and raise the big door at the peak. The pulley system was also used to bring hay into the loft.

My older siblings, Carolyn, Jan, and Ron and the neighboring Blokzyl kids liked to make the pulley rope hang down to a point where they could reach it and hang on. The others would then pull on the rope and hoist the person holding onto the rope way up in the air close to the roof. My sister, Diane, at three years old, would also want to swing on the rope. My siblings agreed and brought the rope down for Diane to hang on to. She was hoisted up in the air and too fast. Her knuckles hit the railing at the top of the barn causing her to let go. Diane fell about 15 feet to the floor and started to cry, holding her arm. She was offered a sucker if she stopped crying and Diane agreed. The Blokzyl kids headed home. Mom was in town getting groceries, so my siblings put Diane down for her nap. Everything went well until Mom went in to get her after her nap. Diane was crying about her arm. Mom saw that her arm was swollen about five times its normal size. She had broken it from her fall and the sucker did not heal the bone. Mom rushed Diane into the doctor and got her on the road to recovery. After Mom got home, she wanted to know what happened. After the incident was explained, Mom used one of her sayings, "You 'dumb ninnies,' you could have killed that girl."

The hayloft was dark. There were only a couple of windows on the front of the barn (as you can see in the first picture) and one in the back (as you can see in the third picture). The sunlight coming in from those windows would create many different shadows in the loft that changed throughout the day. One day, Johnny, Laura, and I were climbing up into the hayloft. In the front corner of the loft there was a shadow that looked like a gorilla squatting and ready to jump at us. We could both see it, and it "scared the living daylights out of us." We shot down the ladder and out of the barn. We had to find something to protect ourselves. I found a pipe and Johnny found a huge rock. We climbed the silo to the point of being able to get on the roof of the barn. It was not easy getting that big pipe and rock onto the roof. We waited and waited for that gorilla to come out and go away. He never did. We must have been on that roof for two hours. It took us a good week before we entered the barn again. We slowly climbed the ladder to the loft and looked to see if the gorilla was still there. It was a different time of day than the first time, so the shadows were all different and there was nothing resembling a gorilla anywhere.

When the silo was empty, we could climb in through the bottom and call out or sing and hear the echo of our voices. Pigeons would nest at the top of the silo where the metal top connected to the cement. Our singing or yelling would cause a lot of flapping as the pigeons escaped the noise. You had to watch out for any ballast they got rid of in their escape. Speaking of pigeons, every pigeon seemed to be full-grown. I saw a lot of other baby birds but do not recall ever seeing a baby pigeon.

Another scary thing about that barn was the spiders. Barn spiders are huge. Since the lighting was low in the barn, we had to be extra careful to avoid running into a large web with a barn spider on it. It was funny to see someone else run into a web. They would do a combination Kung fu and ants in your pants dance followed by, "Do you see a spider on me?" If it were an annoying cousin, I would have a lot of fun with my responses like, "Wow! Not just the big one but a bunch of babies too!

CHAPTER 3
RISKY BEHAVIOR

Every day the animals needed hay. The hay was stored in the hayloft in the upper part of the barn. As you walked halfway into the barn, access to the hayloft was on the left. The ladder to the loft was built on the wall and went up through an opening 3' x 3'. Usually, my sisters would be up in the loft and my brother down below by the animals. One day, my sister Janet asked my brother Ron to toss up the pitchfork. Ron grabbed the pitchfork and threw it up through the hole, prongs first. Well, Jan did not catch it. It then bounced off the roof and came down prongs first. Unfortunately, Ron was looking up with his mouth open when it came back down. The last prong went into Ron's right cheek, out his mouth and nailed him to the ground! Of course, the next stop was Mom and then the doctor! An addendum to the rules was made. No looking up through the opening when tossing anything up and be sure you are out of the way if it should come back down! All through those years we never saw a single gray hair on Mom's head. She and Lady Clairol had bonded!

This next incident happened before I was born. My brother, Ron, was three years old at the time. He either forgot or ignored another rule. No going into the pasture! That was where the bull was. For whatever reason, Ron ventured into the pasture by the barn. The bull was on him in no time. It knocked Ron over onto his back using its head. Ron remembers that huge head looking down at him, snorting and scraping his hooves in the dirt. What was going to happen next? Once again, the house broom came out of nowhere, as far as the bull was concerned. Mom to the rescue! She hit that bull right between the eyes. The bull jumped back and moved away. Mom rescued Ron, held him tight, and reviewed the rules once outside of the pasture.

A lot of lessons can be learned growing up on a farm. Later in life, my wife's sister moved out onto a farm with her husband and their six young children. I remember going out and spending an entire day with the kids pointing out dangers that lurk on the farm. I told them that if they followed the rules, they were less likely to get badly hurt. They were good at keeping the injuries to a minimum. So, the message is to slow down, think things through, and follow the rules. Then you will still have remarkable stories, but fewer scars.

CHAPTER 4

ACK! THE KNIFE

This is a picture of our farm home. These next two stories involve the steps and screen door going into the house. Right beyond the screen door was what we called the porch. It was about 4 feet wide and 6 feet deep with a door at the far end that led into the kitchen. On the bench, to the immediate right when you walked in, was where the milkman would leave one or two cases of milk every Tuesday and Thursday. Beside the milk cases, in the summertime, there was always a small paring knife.

The knife was most often used in one of the gardens to cut flowers or harvest vegetables. Grandpa Fontaine kept the knife sharp!

One summer day when I was six years old, my four-year-old brother, John, turned on me for no reason at all... except for significant teasing. He started chasing me through the house. I dashed through the porch, slammed the screen door, and held it shut. I tried talking to my brother calmly, saying, "Nanna nanna na-na!" John, wanting to scare me, picked up the paring knife and threw it at me, expecting it to bounce off the screen. Well, when it hit the screen, it went point first and it proceeded through the screen and into my forehead! Of course, as in any head wound, there was blood everywhere. I must have been quite a sight when I walked into the kitchen crying for Mom. I looked like something out of a bad horror movie. I do not remember going to the doctor, so my tetanus immunization was up to date, which is important for farm kids. I do remember a lot of soap, hydrogen peroxide, a bandage and Mom holding me tight, crying with me. It is funny, I am feeling that little scar right now. Fortunately, I healed quickly. The next incident happened a few weeks later.

All my brothers and sisters were in the big garden on the other side of the house. One of the things they were doing was harvesting green beans. One of my older siblings told me to run and get the paring knife from the porch. So, I ran into the porch, grabbed the knife, and headed out. As you can see in the picture, there were no railings on the steps. Somehow, probably because I was in a hurry, I tripped and fell off those steps! Are you wondering what happened to the knife? Well, the crash to the ground caused me to stab myself right above my lip and just below my nose. The knife went through and stuck between my upper front two teeth. For a second time, I came into the kitchen crying for Mom. She pulled the knife out, cleaned me up with soap, water, hydrogen peroxide and a tight bandage. Mom held me tight and cried with me. A couple of words that I remember from those moments were "dumb ninny". With seven of us kids doing what kids do, that phrase was common. We came to take it as a term of endearment.

CHAPTER 5
OUR WINDMILL WINDFALL

Our family had one of the last remaining windmills in the area. The windmill had been used to pump water and to create electricity for the batteries at its base. At the time of this story, the windmill was not being used for either. The highway was a quarter of a mile away, allowing neighbors to easily see the windmill and see which direction the wind was blowing. It was a bit of a landmark.

When my brother Ron was 9 or 10 years old, we had a cousin, Paul, who was visiting from out of town. Paul was two years older than Ron and had a desire to start farm machinery and take it for a ride. Those days, all trucks, cars, and machinery had their keys left in them. You never took the keys because someone might need a vehicle or piece of machinery at a moment's notice.

One day, Dad had to leave the farm for a while. Knowing Paul's draw toward machinery, he said to Ron and Paul, "Do not start the machinery!" Well, before long, Paul's desire to drive something overrode Dad's command. He jumped in the truck that was in the yard and turned the key. The truck started but was also in first gear. The truck lurched forward, and Paul decided to drive around the windmill. Ron jumped on the running board of the truck telling Paul to stop. Paul said he was just going to go around the windmill and then stop. As he was going around the far corner of the windmill, (as you see it in the picture,) the truck box caught that bottom leg, causing the whole windmill to tip over and hit the garage. (You see on the right.) It also poked a hole in the roof of the garage. Paul said, "I turned too short!" He ran into the house crying.

The phone started ringing. Neighbors who had driven by were wondering what happened to the windmill. When dad got home, he went into the house to find Paul crying and saying, "I turned too short!" Dad then called our uncle and told him that Paul would be spending another day at the farm. He also explained what had happened. Dad then took the boys outside and gave them each two wrenches. Their job was to disassemble the entire windmill. It took them two days to do the job. Ron said that there were enough nuts and bolts to fill two 5-gallon buckets! They had to neatly stack all the metal angle iron pieces next to the garage. They could not believe there were so many parts to the windmill. There are no more stories about Paul starting at machinery on our farm.

CHAPTER 6
OUR 1956
YELLOWSTONE TRIP

The summer before my dad passed away, he and Mom took us all on a road trip to Yellowstone National Park. It was a wonderful trip from beginning to end. A couple of memories I have about the day of departure was how Mom could pack the car trunk. She organized everything thoughtfully so when it was time to close the trunk, it looked like you could not fit an envelope into it. The second memory was Mom giving me several comic books that were in a brown lunch bag as we were rolling down the road. For some reason, the only comic book I remember is "Baby Huey."

With Dad, Mom, and six kids in a 55 Mercury, we were all in close quarters. The four oldest got the backseat most of the time. Each would take turns having the window seats. Sometimes, Diane, #4 child, sat in the front seat. The front seat was often the seat by the door because Mom loved sitting next to Dad. My younger brother John and I spent most of the time in the front seat, although I do remember sitting on the floor in the back seat reading my comic books. My favorite place was to lay in the back window. Most cars, in that day, did not have air conditioning, so all the other windows would be open creating a nice breeze in the back window.

A portable toilet- well more of a portable toilet seat- was part of our gear. It had a foldable aluminum frame with a toilet seat attached. If nature called beyond a gas station, Dad would pull over by a wooded area and those who needed to go would follow Mom into the woods. I remember Mom scolding my brother John, who was almost 3 years old at the time, for trying the toilet out in our yard. It was just sitting there waiting to be packed by her. Mom could not stay upset with John for long. As

18

soon as she touched the top of his head, she would smile. John's short hair always felt like velvet. She could not help stroking his hair several times and saying, "My John". It also helped that he was the baby of the family at the time.

Yellowstone National Park was quite different back then. Today there are paved pathways and child safe railings. When we were there, there were only wooden planks with no railings. We walked on those boards beside bubbling hot pools just a foot or two away. It was quite an unforgettable sight along with the strong smell of sulfur in the air.

Another thing that was different then were the bears. There were so many bears roaming around. Once we stopped to look at some bears on the other side of the road. Ron and Diane were having their turns at having the window seats. As we were all looking at the big bears through Ron's side, a big bear cub came up to Diane's side and stuck its head through the window opening. Ron noticed it first and yelled "Diane!" Diane turned and came face-to-face with the bear cub! There was much screaming while Ron reached over and rolled up the window. The screams scared the bear worse than he had scared us. When talking to Diane to verify my facts, she told me that her husband, Ray, had a similar experience last fall when he came face-to-face with a large black bear while bow hunting. I had to chuckle and comment that they both now have had close encounters with bears.

CHAPTER 7
YELLOWSTONE
TRIP CONTINUED

SEPT. 1956

SEPT. 1956

On our Yellowstone National Park trip in 1956, we traveled cross country from Minnesota. We had a 1955 Mercury that pulled a small pop-up trailer. The trailer only had a double bed in it. Dad and Mom slept in the bed, and John and I slept on the floor beside the bed. Carolyn, Jan, Ron, and Diane slept in a five-person tent. The tent did not have a floor like the tents of today, so the ground had to be cleared before you laid out your sleeping bags.

Yellowstone Park trash cans were buried in the ground and had heavy metal lids. Each lid had a lever type pedal that allowed you to open the lid and deposit your trash. The heavy lids kept the small critters out, but not the bears. When you took your foot off the lid pedal, the heavy lid would slam down with a loud clang. Throughout the night you heard the bears coming through the campground checking the trash. All night we heard clang, clang, clang. It was a little unnerving. The trash cans were an engineering idea that was obviously not tested.

One night Dad, Mom, John, and I were awakened by the rocking of our trailer. It was a significant rocking of that small trailer. It was a big bear scratching his back on the rear left corner of our trailer. Dad had a big flashlight that had a white lens on the front and a red light on the top. He turned on the red light and waved it out the back of the canvas opening on the trailer. It did the trick. The bear stopped scratching his back and walked away toward the older kids' tent. As the bear was sniffing around the tent, he woke up my brothers and sisters. The bear came to the screen opening sniffing around. Fear filled the tent…

At previous campsites, we had seen what bears could do. Dad had been warned not to carry any processed meat in our coolers, such as bacon, ham, etc. One afternoon, a big brown bear walked right through our campsite into the campsite next to ours. The campers there had a big red Coca-Cola locking cooler. Its handle snapped over the top of the cooler locking the lid in place. It was a very sturdy cooler. Well, that bear treated that big cooler like a thin cardboard box. He threw it up in the air, pounced on it, and proceeded to tear the cooler apart. It was an amazing thing to witness. After the bear had gotten what it wanted, it left. Dad went over to talk to the man in the next campsite and asked what was in the cooler. The man said bacon and eggs! That camper learned the hard way about processed meats and bears.

In another campground, a bear came into the campsite next to ours. The bear went after a big purse on the picnic table. The lady who owned it was not happy. She had her brand-new Polaroid camera in that purse. Her husband had to hold her back from going after her purse. In the purse was a Hershey bar. That was what the bear was after. The bear tore the purse apart like a wet paper bag. Fortunately, he was not into photography and took only the Hershey bar, then walked away.

So, back to the kids' tent and the bear. Tent canvas is much thinner than a metal cooler. My brother and sisters were not processed meat but meat, nonetheless. The many bears roaming around the campsite that night had everyone on edge. As the bear was sniffing around the tent, my brother, Ron, started crawling toward the entrance of the tent. My sisters asked where he was going and he said, "Out of the tent!" My sisters said, "Don't go out there! You will be eaten!" Ron said, "I don't care, I have to throw up!" The bear had walked away by the time Ron got outside and did what he needed to do. It was fortunate that none of them had a BLT before going to bed.

Dad snapped the picture of Mom, John, and me in the trailer after the bear left. Can you tell by the eyes that John takes after Mom's side of the family? From that night on, Mom insisted we stay in cabins rather than a campsite. I am sure the feeling was unanimous.

CHAPTER 8

THUNDER AND LIGHTNING STORMS

Thunder and lightning storms were a thing of awe when I was a kid. Often, the air would turn an eerie lime green before the storm came through. Everything would be dead quiet. You did not hear a peep from the birds. With the landscape being so flat in our area, you could see the storm rolling in. Watching the lightning approach was exciting and a little fearful. The thunder was incredible. We would always say there was a baseball game going on between the angels in heaven. Depending on the loudness of the crack of thunder, we would determine whether it was a bunt, foul ball, base hit, double, triple, or home run. We enjoyed officiating the game. The migrant family next to us had a great fear of these types of storms. They would often show up before the storm hit to ask us if they could stay in our basement until the storm passed. Like the birds, there was never a peep out of them while they were in the basement.

It was always fun seeing the lightning and then counting until you heard the thunder. That would tell us how far away the lightning had struck. Our eyes would get big when the time gap was one second or less. That meant lightning struck within a mile of our house. Many times, the lightning and thunder would go on for a long time. Our dog, Penny, was not allowed to go beyond the throw rug at the kitchen entrance. So, one of us would often sit with her and pet her when she would shake with fear.

One night while we were all sleeping, lightning hit the silo five times in succession. The big cement silo was empty. The thunderclaps were the loudest we had ever heard. It sat every one of us straight up in bed when that happened. It was like a cannon had gone off in our bedroom. We all got up and looked out the window at the silo. The top three rings (that banded the silo and were about 3 feet apart), were all glowing red. We learned the next day that the lightning strikes broke the concrete at the base of the silo. The energy from those lightning strikes entered the house and fried every outlet and light switch. Our fuse box in the basement had every one of the fuses blown out of the box, and they were laying in the corner of the shower 18 feet across the room. Mr. Erickson, from Erickson Electric, was out the next day. He had never seen anything like it and was surprised that there was not a fire. He had to replace every outlet and switch in the house. He had also never seen fuses blown out of the fuse box like that. He replaced the fuses and got us up and running. It was that lightning strike that motivated Dad to have lightning rods installed on all the farm buildings.

I would have loved to have been the lightning rod salesman when that product was introduced to all the farmers. Nearly every homestead had lightning rods installed on each important building. I learned later that Benjamin Franklin invented the lightning rod. He figured it was a way to move the energy of a lightning bolt to the ground rather than through the building. As you can see in the picture, the lightning rods had aluminum cables that went from rod to rod and then down the side of the building to a metal rod hammered deep into the ground. Although well-prepared, we were never hit by lightning again.

Our family often did a lot of praying during the storms. The greatest fear from a storm was hail. Hailstorms could wipe out a crop in minutes. That happened to us in 1950. In those days, before hybridization, stalks of grain would grow very tall. The wheat was so tall in the fields you could not see the top of my dad's head as he ventured out into them. The heads of wheat were 7 to 8 inches long and it looked like a bumper crop which would create a high yield. A violent looking storm was approaching. The sky had rolling colors of green and gray. The clouds looked like bubble wrap and were dark and ominous. Dad said to Ron, "Ronnie let's go look at our crop because I don't think it will be here tomorrow." Dad and Ron walked out into the field to take one last look. The storm did not last long but it was long enough to destroy the entire crop. The hailstorm had a swath that was about 5 miles wide and 15 miles long. Many of the hailstones were softball size. It destroyed our grain crops and those of most of our neighbors. Fortunately, the sugar beet crop was not wiped out. That saved the farmers from a total loss for that year. The next day, Dad drove the 1950 Mercury he had bought prior to the storm, into Saul Motors in town. He told Mr. Saul, the dealership owner, his crop had been wiped out and he could not afford the car at this time. Mr. Saul said, "Roy, don't worry about it. I know you are good for it. Go home." Of course, Dad was good for it. He paid for it later in the year and bought a new truck from him the next year. You do not hear many stories of customer relationships like that today.

One of my early memories of Dad was during another hailstorm. I was four years old and was sitting on the cement steps going up to the porch door. I was watching Dad walk out into the barley field which was behind the granary. The granary is the first building on the left in the picture.

It started to hail. Dad came running out of the field and towards me. I could hear him singing as he got close to me. "It's hailing, it's hailing, we better get inside, its hailing!" He scooped me up and carried me into the house. That time the hail damaged but did not wipe out the crop.

Thanks, Brother Ron, for clarifying some of the details of these stories.

CHAPTER 9
GRANDPA'S GIRLS

The picture at the top is of Grandpa Cournia with his girls. The ones on Grandpa's left are his daughters and the two on the right are Aunt Lorraine and Mom, his daughters-in-law. Uncle Sonny was not married at the time of this picture, so Aunt Nancy is not in the picture. This picture also does not include Aunt Donna, another daughter, and the aunts from Grandpa's second marriage. Grandma Ann died before I was born. A few years later he married Grandma Jenny. That added several more girls to the mix. I loved them all. It always surprised me how different each aunt was from one another. Each had a very distinct personality. Half of the aunts lived close and the other half at least one state away. Family reunions were always fun to be a part of. The get-togethers were usually out at Grandpa Cournia's farm. When we all got together, there were cousins everywhere. It was difficult to play "Kick the can" because just when you thought you found a good hiding spot, there was an older cousin or two already there. Of course, they would kick you out and tell you to find a different spot. Too often I got caught while I was trying to find a good hiding spot.

Occasionally, in the summer, we would gather at Uncle Bernard and Aunt Esther's (directly on Grandpa's left and the oldest daughter) at the lake in Perham, Minnesota. Other times we would gather at Maple Lake or Union Lake, 30 miles down the road. Going to the lake was always a highlight. It was exciting when we got close enough to smell the lake. That was always a mile or two before we arrived at the lake. Uncle Del and Aunt Lorraine had the first boat and motor that I recall. The boat had a 30 hp Johnson motor, which was powerful enough to pull us around the lake on a knee board. Those were great times.

Aunt Loretta (second daughter from Grandpa) and Uncle Doc lived in town. Uncle Doc was the fire chief. That was cool. He had a separate phone in his house that he could pick up and listen to any emergency call that went into the fire station. Their house was painted fire engine red. You could always tell if Uncle Doc was in the room by his distinctive laugh. In fact, each of the Cournia boys had a very distinctive laugh that gave them away in any crowd. I can hear them now and miss them.

The picture at the bottom is from my brother John's wedding. Most of my aunts and uncles were in attendance. It was a fun evening. A lot of dancing and loud music. In this picture I am dancing with my mom. She loved to dance. But this story focuses on Aunt Nancy, who was the last girl to join Grandpa's girls. Aunt Nancy, Uncle Sonny and family lived less than 2 miles from us. I saw a lot of that family. I worked for a summer or two for Uncle Sonny. It was always a pleasure to walk into Aunt Nancy's kitchen. She was always so cheerful (and still is) when I would come into her presence. I knew her the best and, consequently, she became my favorite Aunt. At John's wedding, all the aunts were sitting around a big round table. I went over to talk to Aunt Nancy at that table. I was down on one knee trying to talk with her. The band was very loud, making it difficult to hear each other. One of the things I said to her was, "You have always been my favorite Aunt!" Aunt Nancy said, "What?" I raised my voice significantly and said the same thing and at the same moment the music stopped. I remember looking around the table and seeing all the other Aunts staring at me. They all had heard what I said and none of them were smiling. All I could do was give them was an "And all of you are my second favorite!" smile.

I often wondered what it was like for Dad, Uncle Del, and Uncle Sonny growing up with eight sisters. That is a lot of estrogen. I had three sisters in the house. It is no wonder us Cournia boys grew up well balanced with the ups and downs of relationships.

CHAPTER 10
HAIRCUTS AND MARIA

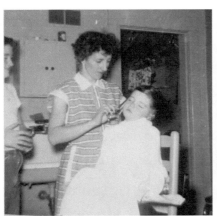

Mom cut our hair until we were about eight years old. I wanted my hair a little longer than my brother John's hair. So, I had more of a scissor cut than a buzz cut and as you can see in the picture, I found haircuts to be boring. John received a full buzz cut. John's short hair always felt like velvet. Mom loved his widow's peak and the feel of his hair. She always smiled when she touched it.

John also tanned darker than anyone else in the family. By mid-summer he looked very Hispanic. The Henry Laura family, who worked in our fields every summer, had a son whom we called Baldo. Baldo was the same age and size as John and had the same haircut. By mid-summer John and Baldo looked like twin brothers. You had to look closely to tell who was who. Uncle Del told us of a time when he was working on a roof at one of the houses of the workers. A car pulled up and a Hispanic family of eight or nine kids piled out of the car. He heard, "Hi, Uncle Del!" He said he looked the group over and could not figure out who had said that, until John said it again and waved at the same time. Even then, he had to look closely to make sure it was John.

As kids, we had so much fun playing with the Laura kids. We were over at their cabin every day. Johnny Laura was my age and we played nonstop. There was Johnny and me, John and Baldo, and their little sister, Lily, who tagged along. One summer Johnny and I each received a Zorro outfit as a gift. In our minds, we saved many villages and damsels in distress.

There were many things that amazed us about that family. Johnny could run like the wind. I had never seen anyone run so amazingly fast. The oldest in the Laura family was Tony. He was tall, good-looking with black wavy hair, and drove a 1957 red Thunderbird convertible, like the one in the picture. I am sure Tony turned many young ladies' heads. One day I was looking at his car and noticed that he had a big open bag of M&Ms by the shifter. I stuck my head in the window on the passenger side

34

looking at the interior and the M&Ms. I was deciding whether to take some M&Ms. All at once, from inside the house, Tony yelled, "Mike! Get out of my car!" That startled me so much that I started to stand up before I got my head out of the car. I hit my head hard on that removable hardtop. Tony saved me from a life of crime.

The Laura family had two older daughters, China, and Maria. I had a crush on Maria. China was also pretty, and she had developed the ability to remove a pop bottle cap with her teeth. It was interesting but not particularly attractive. Anyway, Maria had captured this seven or eight-year-old's heart. One day I was walking along the gravel road by our farm. I started singing a popular song of the day. The song was by Little Peggy March and was called "I Will Follow Him". I sang it a little differently by inserting the word "her" for "him". It was a simple song, and I knew all the words. I belted out that song at least two or three times on that walk. Unbeknownst to me, Maria and her family were working in the beet field less than a quarter mile away. They heard me quite clearly. That evening when I was over at their house playing with Johnny, Maria asked me, "Mike, who were you singing about today?" I must have turned as red as Tony's car. Maria, who was twice my age, knew I had a crush on her. She said, "That was a very nice song, and any girl would love hearing you sing it." I did not know whether to melt or run. The rest of her family took many opportunities to tease me about it. I did not care because it had pleased her.

CHAPTER 11
MOM AS A LITTLE GIRL

This story is about my mom when she was a little girl. Yesterday, I listened to a recording I made in 1994, of Mom retelling these stories. It was wonderful hearing her voice again. Mom had a younger brother, Jim , and a younger sister named Theresa. Theresa drowned at age 2. Grandpa and Grandma Fontaine had a home on the river. They used water from the river for the garden and to wash clothes. They had a makeshift dock that went out into the river. Grandma would go out on that dock with a pail to fetch water. Little Theresa, wanting to mimic her mother, took the pail one day and went out on the dock. When she dipped the pail, the current pulled her in. Grandma ran into the river, up to her neck, trying to save her. Grandma did not know how to swim; she got to Theresa, but it was too late. We were fortunate we did not lose Grandma that day also.

Grandma had a large garden and grew all kinds of produce. Whatever produce was ready each day, Grandma loaded it into a wagon. Mom and Uncle Jim would go all over Crookston selling the produce. Mom remembered doing that for at least three years. Mom was seven years old at the time and Uncle Jim was five years old. Mom said they went all over town and into every neighborhood. They sold all the produce that Grandma packed into their wagon each day. Grandma would give Mom a quarter for her efforts. Mom loved the job and getting paid. Those were different days when you could trust the town folk around your children. Mom learned an excellent work ethic that she carried with her throughout her life. She was always productive. During one of my mom's visits to Oregon, my sister-in-law, who also had six kids, asked Mom if she ever felt like she was spinning her wheels. Mom said, "No, I didn't have time to spin my wheels." It is true if, you exclude Mom spinning her wheels as she left the yard. We would tease her by telling her we could hear the pea rock hitting the barn when she left the yard.

Another thing Mom and Uncle Jim loved to do was to go to the hobo camps by the railroad tracks. She said the hobos had marvelous stories to tell. She learned the differences between a hobo, a tramp, and a bum. The hobos and tramps were men who were looking for work and were using the railroad as their transportation to get from town to town. The bums were drifters, lazy, and untrustworthy. Each man knew what they were and had a certain pride in it. The hobos, during that time, tended to be family men who had a wife and kids in other states. They were out looking for work to support them. The tramps tended to be without a wife or family.

Mom grew up during the depression. It was not easy to get her to talk about those days. When she did, it was usually something positive. Unless you did the math, you would not know that Mom had lived through the Depression. Her parents, my Grandpa and Grandma, were a little different story. But that story is for another time.

Our daughter, Jennie, was so pleased to hear when she was a little girl, that she looked like her grandma. In the first picture, if it were not for the clothes, you would be hard-pressed to determine if it were Jennie or her grandma at that age.

CHAPTER 12

MOM'S COOKING
AND DRIVING

Mom, Aunt Nancy, and Aunt Lorraine would take turns feeding the men that worked the farms. There could easily be over 20 hungry mouths to feed, depending on the season. If the men were working in a field close to the farmhouse, they would gather in the yard (like the picture on the left) to have their meals. If the fields were further away, which was most of the time, the meals would be brought in the trunk of a car. Again, depending on the season, the men were served 2 to 3 meals every day. I remember my mom having big roasters full of hot food and always a different dessert at each meal. There was always coffee, Kool-Aid, and water available. After my wife,

Barbara, and I were married, we asked mom for recipes for some of her fabulous meals. We always chuckled when we got them because many of the recipes served 25 to 50 people! How do you cut that down to serve two?

As an aside, the picture on the left taken outside our home, shows the big sandbox in the background. That is the sandbox where the rooster attacked me. Uncle Sonny (who is on Mom's left wearing the hat with the turned-up bill) was the one who first chased the rooster and ended up getting chased by the rooster. Uncle Sonny is also leaning against the car in the picture on the right. His legs (pictured here) are what they looked like when the rooster was chasing him – out in front of his body.

Mom did not get her driver's license until after Dad died. The absence of a driver's license did not stop Mom from delivering food to the men in the distant fields. Maybe because Mom was in a hurry to get the hot meal delivered, she drove fast. We always chuckled when Mom drove out of the yard. We told her we could hear the pea rock ricocheting off the barn as she peeled out. Grandpa Cournia was often on Mom's case about how fast she drove. He said he could see her coming from more than a mile away. Mom created quite a rooster tail of dust on those gravel roads.

I learned my "peppy" driving from my mom. I bought my first car when I was 14 years old and could drive it on the country roads but not into town. I failed my first driver's test due to the poor habits I had developed over the previous years. I had four points deducted for driving with my right hand on the steering wheel and my left arm relaxed on the door with the window down. To me, the 10 o'clock and 2 o'clock positions were only used in more tense conditions. Mom had a more challenging time getting her driver's license. She failed the driving test three times. You never have to parallel park or turn your wheel toward the curb on a hill when you live on a farm. She drove too fast and with one hand also, because the other was used as a temporary seatbelt for us kids in the front seat when she would hit the brakes. When Mom took her fourth driving test, she drove to and from the courthouse in the family car. The same guy always did the driving tests. When Mom would leave after failing the test, he would ask her where she was going. Mom would say, "Home! I have men to feed." He would say, "You can't do that because you don't have a license" as she was driving away.

CHAPTER 13

THE COURNIA SINGERS

Mom loved to sing. She had an amazing voice. She and my sisters, Carolyn, Janet, and Diane used to do many singing performances. They were often featured on the radio singing their hearts out. Mom was so proud of them. I wish I had a recording of Mom and the girls singing.

Mom also sang solo on many occasions. Sometimes she was featured on the radio and other times with friends at the large dinner parties that were common in those days. Many of Mom and Dad's friends have told me over the years how they would always ask Mom to sing. Someone would usually say, "Eleanor, please get up and sing!" Mom's two favorite songs to sing were

"Ave Maria" and "Indian Love Call." I am sure Dad beamed every time she sang. Fortunately, I have a vinyl record of Mom singing. I need to have it digitalized so that any of the next generations can hear her sing.

There was always music in the house. Most often it was Mom humming. She was usually too busy to sit down at the piano and accompany herself. My wife, Barbara, also has a beautiful voice. Daily, I hear her humming some beautiful songs. It always brings a smile to my face, and it reminds me of Mom. I love it when she plays the piano and sings. Our dog, Theodore, who is gone now, loved to hear her play and sing. I would be playing with him in another room, having a fun time, when Barbara would start playing the piano. Theodore would stop playing, his eyes would widen, he would leave the room, and go and lay down behind her at the piano. There was no moving him from that spot until Barbara was done. I understood why. It also helped that Barbara told him, every day, that he was "the best dog in the whole world."

Mom's singing style was more traditional and classical. Being a high soprano contributed to that. It always gave us pause when she would come out with a unique style. She could sound like Ella Fitzgerald and other great jazz singers of the time. Dad's nickname for Mom was "Tops." I often wondered if it came from the Cole Porter song, "You're the Top." Mom surely was the top.

Mom even broke out in a Beatles song one day. That surprised me. It was after she told me a joke. "What is an octopus's favorite song?" Answer, "I want to hold your hand hand hand hand hand hand hand hand!" She enjoyed their music, even if "they needed a haircut."

43

CHAPTER 14
GRADE SCHOOL DAYS

Third grade, for some reason, is where I have the most memories of my time at Cathedral Grade School. I have memories from all the grades, but there is quite a thick file from third grade. Kindergarten, apart from my dad dying that November, was a wonderful experience. Sister Maureen was our teacher. She was incredibly kind, supportive, and encouraging. One of the vivid memories from kindergarten was getting to be milk monitor.

Every day we had a break and were given a glass bottle of milk. You could have chocolate or white milk. The milk bottles had a foil cap (pictured) that needed to have a hole punched in it to make room for the straw. The milk monitor was the one who got to punch the hole in each cap. We all looked forward to that job. The other vivid memory was who ordered white milk instead of chocolate. There were just two, Paul Fontaine and Evelyn Altepeter. They were also the two that I remember getting sick in class. My reasoning, as a five-year-old, was that they got sick because they chose white milk. It made sense at the time.

Our third-grade teacher was Sister Charlotte, and she was okay. She had the unique ability to make a "tsk" sound with her tongue and the roof of her mouth and could be heard clearly over a long distance. That is how she got our attention. She was born and raised in Barnesville, Minnesota and she never lets us forget how nice Barnesville was. On her days off, there were times I wished she would move back to Barnesville. But she was committed to my education.

That year, I was smitten by an extremely cute classmate, Connie Raymond. She was the first girl I ever gave a gift to. My sister, Diane, gave me a charm bracelet she no longer wore. I found a little box that had a bed of cotton on the bottom, snuggled the bracelet into the box, and wrapped it up. When Connie opened the gift, she was excited and called me "a living doll." I told this story to my wife, Barbara, before we were even married. To this day, with a twinkle in her eye, she will occasionally call me "a living doll." In those days, messages to each of us were delivered by our best friends. Connie's best friend was Janelle Braun and mine was Greg Proulx. One day, I had a plan to meet Connie around the corner of the school to give her a first kiss. Messages went back and forth by Janelle and Greg and a date and time was set. It had to be during recess because that was the only time it was possible to be alone. I was "looking forward" to that recess. You have heard the term "Loose lips sink ships." Well, when the time came, we met at the designated spot only to find most of the rest of our class waiting there to observe the kiss. Neither Connie nor I were ready for center stage. We both walked away, embarrassed, and I was extremely disappointed.

Another memory about Connie was when I turned in a homework assignment. Sister Charlotte pulled me aside the next day and showed me the paper I had turned in. She pointed to where my name was, but it said Mike Connie rather than Mike Cournia. I had no recollection of doing that and did not own up to it. Sister Charlotte gave me a good scolding and sent me on my way. Another time, after school and during the winter, I was showing off on the sidewalk close to where Connie was sitting in her dad's new blue Chevy. I had my hockey stick and a chunk of ice that was a little bigger than a hockey puck. I was going to show Connie how good my slapshot was. I was aiming for the street in front of their car, but my aim was off, and the ice chunk hit Mr. Raymond's car. He was a tall man, and when he got out of his car, he looked even taller. He scolded me right there about 3 feet from the car. Connie was watching the whole thing. There was no damage to the car and I profusely apologized. He graciously accepted my apology and got back into the car. I walked away, embarrassed, and extremely disappointed.

The following spring, Greg and I got into trouble one afternoon. Central high school (the third picture} was directly across the street from our grade school and high school. Grade school kids were released at the end of the day before high school. Greg and I crossed the street and went over to those ground-level windows you see in the picture. Being a warm, sunny day, all the windows were open. Those were sunken classrooms. Greg and I would sneak up to the windows and stick our heads into a classroom and yell out, "Class dismissed!" We should have stopped after doing it twice. The third time Greg stuck his head in and dismissed the class, the teacher was standing beside the window with his back against the wall. He grabbed Greg and pulled him inside. The next day Greg and I had to stand before our principal, Sister DeChantal, and receive a long and forceful scolding. When Sister DeChantal was really upset her eyelids would quiver like they do when you bite into a lemon. Her eyelids quivered like that from the beginning to the end of the scolding. We were in big trouble. That scolding kept us both from becoming juvenile delinquents. Shortly after that, Connie had Janelle give me back the charm bracelet. She saw no future with the juvenile delinquent.

Another memory from that year were the raffles the nuns would have. They were raising money to help save pagan babies. They never called it a raffle, but we were able to buy "chances" to win a prize. Often it was a glow-in-the-dark baby Jesus or Crucifix which brought in the most money. I wondered about those pagan babies and how they ended up.

Sister Charlotte would occasionally read a book to us during class. My favorite was "The Good Bad Boy." I related a lot to the boy in the story. The boy ends up becoming a priest in the book. That sounded reasonable because I wanted to become a priest up until third grade.

Our grade school was right behind our high school (pictured). The back half was the nun's residence. There were three access points to their residence: in the back through the kitchen, a formal entrance on the side, or through swinging doors by the water fountain on the second floor. Occasionally, I got a glimpse when a nun would come through one of the swinging doors. I never saw more than a hallway with many doors, but it was intriguing. It was off-limits to any student. As far as I know, no one ever broke that law. One day I was excused from class to go to the bathroom. I was told to be quick about it. I was quickly returning to class, and while I was coming around the corner by the water fountain, I collided with Sister Eulalia as she was hurrying, just as fast, to get back to her class. She was a young and pretty nun, and I was worried that I had hurt her. She stepped back, caught her breath, and then burst out laughing. I have never seen a nun laugh so hard. She finally stopped laughing and asked if I was okay. We then went our separate ways. A nun's habit, in those days took away most body form. As they walked, they appeared to move like hovercraft. You did not see their feet much, just their glide. Up until that day I had really never thought that nuns were a traditional woman. That collision changed my thinking.

CHAPTER 15
THE BASEMENT

Our basement on the farm was a typical unfinished basement. In its several rooms, it contained a huge old-style oil furnace, an oil tank to fuel the furnace, an old-style fuse box, a gigantic chest freezer, a large shower, a water heater, pressure tank, ping-pong table, and many mousetraps. While playing hide and seek, it was unwise to forget about the mousetraps. Several times I got my toes snapped while wearing only socks or footed pajamas. It was easy to find the person who was hiding after they triggered a mousetrap.

The stairs going down to the basement were also used as a disciplinary tool. If one of us had done something that warranted a timeout due to our behavior, we would have to sit on one of the stairs in the dark. Depending on the level of infraction, you were told which stair you had to sit on. That was no fun. At about the fourth or fifth stair down, you could no longer see the light from under the basement entrance door. So, you hoped you never had to sit below those stairs. It was unimaginable to have to sit on the bottom stair. I am sure I never achieved that level of infraction, although my brother Ron was a frequent resident of the bottom stairs. (I am sure those of you who know Ron are not surprised by that fact. ☺) We had to sit on our assigned stair for a certain length of time. We could not get up too early, or our time was lengthened. If we spent the appropriate amount of time, we could come up and sit next to Dad. He would ask us if we had learned our lesson. If we had a repentant heart, Dad would smile and then allow us to go about our business. It was an effective deterrent.

The door to the basement stairs was off the den. My brother John fell off the left side of those stairs when he was about five years old. None of us knew that it had happened. Mom came into the den on that day and asked me where John was. I said he was playing in the basement and that you could hear him playing with a toy truck. I thought he was making truck sounds, but he was moaning due to the fall. Mom could tell it was not a truck sound and went down and scooped John up and took him to the doctor. Our job was to keep John awake. He had had a concussion. Everything turned out okay.

The chest freezer was about 6 feet long, 3 1/2 feet high, and 2 feet wide. With a family our size, it was needed freezer space. The only mishap that I know of was when my sister Carolyn was sent down to get something out of the freezer. When she opened the freezer, there was a big pig's head that had come unwrapped. Our grandma liked to make head cheese from that part of the pig. Well, Carolyn saw the pig's head and fainted dead away. Someone was sent down to find out what was taking Carolyn so long. There she was, lying next to the freezer, unconscious. She was revived and it was never mentioned again. Maybe.

The water pressure tank was in the room that was in the southwest corner of the basement. That was the canning cellar. Being the canning cellar, it was filled with all kinds of canned goods in glass jars. One time, the pressure tank blew up and went through the wall into the next room where it took out the water heater. There were a few jars broken. I often wondered why we were supposed to go to that room during a tornado. I do not know if it was an old wives' tale or what, but if you are in a house with a basement during a tornado, you are to go to the southwest corner. I would look in that room and see the canning jars, pressure tank, and wonder if that was really the safest place to be!

The only time we were not allowed to go down in the basement was when Mom was wrapping Christmas presents. Of course, that is when we wanted to go down there the most. Mom used the ping-pong table to lay out the presents and wrap them using a tremendous amount of Scotch tape. We always kidded Mom about the amount of Scotch tape she used.

Showering in the basement was a little uncomfortable. It was usually chilly after you turned off the shower. Also, you had to watch out for the bigger spiders. That taught me alertness!

Before Mom got a clothes dryer, the basement was used to hang frozen laundry that had come from the outside clothesline in the dead of winter. The basement was multifaceted. It was a place that none of us kids will ever forget. Especially those times when we were playing in the basement and one of my siblings would "accidentally" turn off the lights.

CHAPTER 16
PENNY

Farm pets differed from farm to farm. Ours were mostly dogs. I have only one memory of cats on our farm. One day two barn kittens got into the house. Mom chased after them because no animals were allowed in the house. As Mom chased the cats, they chose Mom's nice drapes as an escape route. They really tore up the drapes in their attempted escape. I remember her finally catching them and throwing them outside. It might have been that incident that gives a reason I have no other memories of cats on our farm.

When the older kids were young, they had two dogs, Butch and Tippy. Tippy is in the picture with Diane. Butch was a big cattle dog. When it was time for milking, all he had to be told was, "Butch, go get the cows." Off he would go and get the cows to the barn. Tippy was small when compared to Butch. I loved hearing the stories about those two dogs when they were fighting off another animal that had come into the yard. Tippy would stand between Butch's front legs in those types of fights. I understand they never lost.

Most of my pet memories are of our Pennys. We had three consecutive Pennys. The first two were the same breed, Samoyed, and were great pets. The Penny that is in the right picture always stayed closest to John. Mom loved the fact that if she wanted to know where John was on the farm, she would call, "Penny!" and Penny would come into view from somewhere in the farmyard. From that, she always knew where John was. One of the reasons Penny stayed close to John was that John often shared his food with her. He would even share a sucker or ice cream cone with her. He would take a couple licks, then Penny would take a couple licks.

Barn swallows came with every farm. They were fun to watch but were dirty nesters. When you got close to where their nest was, they would start divebombing you. The swallows, especially, did not like Penny. If she got anywhere close to the building they nested in, they would get aggressive with her. One day I watched Penny walking along the granary. A couple of swallows started diving at her. I was so surprised when all at once she grabbed one of them out of the air. I did not know she could be so fast. She really missed us when we were on our family trip to Yellowstone. When we got home, Mom opened her car door and all at once, Penny leapt into the front seat, laid flat and cried like a baby. All our hearts melted with her joy. The first Penny's downfall was when she chased cars and trucks as they were leaving the farmyard. She was hit and killed by an electrician's pickup truck as he was leaving.

The next Penny had the same temperament as the first. She also stuck close to John. That Penny liked to lay on the snowbank in front of our picture window in the winter. The snowbank was usually the same height as the bottom of the window, and she would watch us from outside. Being completely white, she blended in with the snowbank to the point that we would not see her until she opened her eyes. She eventually earned the right to sleep on the rug by the back door. Occasionally, Mom would catch Penny crawling from that rug to the den. If she made it to the den, she would beat feet upstairs to be with John. One summer we took a trip to California. Grandpa and Grandma Fontaine watched over the farm and fed Penny. Grandpa called Penny "One Red Cent." While we were away Grandpa thought Penny would be more comfortable if he gave her a type of poodle cut. When we got home, poor Penny was very sunburned. We were all upset that Grandpa had done that. John would not talk to Grandpa for weeks. This Penny died after a fight with a monster pack rat. This rat was about 4 feet long, had a 2-foot body and a 2-foot tail. It was a horrendous fight. Penny killed the rat, but the rat ended up killing Penny through infection.

The last Penny was a Spitz rather than a Samoyed. She was fun while she was a puppy but got a little squirrelly as she got older.

We had to put her down after she had attacked me. One day I was over by the chicken coop which was attached to the granary. I saw Penny start to shake and then fall to her side. It looked like she was having a seizure. When she got back on her feet, she started to growl at me like she was a wolf. I knew I was in significant danger. The word "rabies" immediately came to mind. I took off running toward the house yelling, "open the door!" Penny was chasing me like she was a wild animal. John happened to be in the screened porch when this happened and opened and closed the door as I dove into the screened porch. Penny crashed into the door. She continued that behavior all around the house. She finally got herself wedged behind the propane tanks and everything went quiet. We did not dare go outside for quite a while. When we did go out, we had a gun and had to have an "Old Yeller" moment when we found her.

John and I had a pet goat for about a week. It was a young white goat that I found walking down the road by the farmhouse. So, I brought it home and asked Mom if we could keep it. She said we could until we found out who it belonged to. We could not find anyone who even had a goat, much less had lost one. The young goat was happy to be around us. He lost favor with Mom when he started eating her flowers. The goat did not heed her warnings. One day when John and I were walking home from a day of playing with the Hanson boys, we saw a white goatskin hanging on the fence by our migrant workers' house. We ran home to tell Mom that that family had killed our goat. Mom told us, "No. I gave it to them. He got into my flower beds one too many times." Mom was extremely sensitive about her flowerbeds. The only time we ever heard her say a foul word was when one of the dogs was digging in her flower bed. She came to the door and yelled out, "Get that damn dog out of my flower bed!" We were all stunned. That was the only time we heard her say a foul word. That taught us a permanent fact: you do not mess with Mom's flowers.

CHAPTER 17
SLIDING AND SEWING

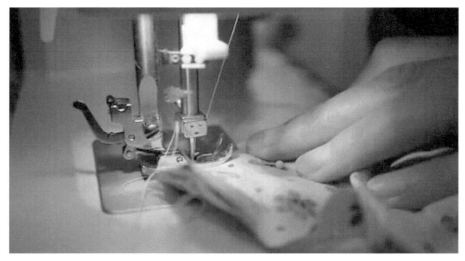

One of the exciting things to do on the farm was to slide down the granary roof. The roof was covered with corrugated metal held in with nails that had something like tar washers under the heads of the nails. That washer helped resist water getting in the nail hole. As you can see in the granary picture, we had quite a slope on either side. The left side did not drop as much as the right side. The right side had a type of ladder attached to the roof. It made it easy to climb to the top. The left side was preferable to slide on in the summer because it gave us a better chance to stop before the end of the roof. In the wintertime, it did not matter because we were usually sliding into a snowbank.

As a roof ages, the nails tend to loosen and stick up about an eighth of an inch or so. In the summertime we had a twofold focus. One was to miss the nails that stuck up and the other was to stop before the end of the roof. By the time John and I were old enough to climb to the top and slide down, there were quite a few nails sticking up. As we slid down the roof, we would have to lift a foot here a leg there or our bottom in another spot. We were not always successful. Mom would scold us for ripping our jeans or overalls on those nails. She sewed up quite a few pairs of jeans during the summer. It was the same in the winter, just different clothes. In the wintertime we had snow suits that would snag on the nails, it usually made bigger tears in that type of fabric than in jeans.

The fun usually stopped when one of us would be bleeding due to a nail catching one of our hands, feet, or behind. The focus on the nails diminished the closer we got to the end of the roof. I remember one time when a nail caught my shorts and kept me from going off the end of the roof. So, the nails were not all bad.

In the wintertime the sliding was fast. The right side of the granary was especially fast due to its pitch. It was most fun when the snowbank was soft when we flew off the edge of the roof. In the summertime, the roof could be hot which diminished our focus on the two main challenges.

Mom was an expert sewer. She could easily fix our torn jeans or cutoffs or snow suits. Before Mom got her electric sewing machine, she had a treadle Singer sewing machine just like the one in the picture. Her feet were the motor for the machine. It was quite amazing to watch. The sewing machine was in the den where she had a big built-in cupboard with shelves of fabric. If one of my sisters needed a new dress, they would pick out a pattern and then the fabric. If I remember correctly, patterns were only $.10 in those days. Mom could whip out a dress in an afternoon. She really liked creating with the sewing machine.

Back to the old treadle sewing machine, my brothers and sisters would try to mimic Mom and her sewing. None of them were tall enough to run the treadle and feed the fabric at the same time. Like driving Grandpa Fontaine's car, they had to work together to accomplish the task. One would be on the floor rocking the treadle to make the machine go and one would be up feeding the fabric. One time my brother was feeding the fabric a little too fast and managed to get his finger under the descending needle. The needle went right through his finger. Ron's sewing ability after that was just sew – sew.

CHAPTER 18
EARLY DRIVING

Grandpa and Grandma Fontaine would often come out to the farm for a visit on Sunday afternoons. The usual scenario included Dad, Mom, Grandpa and Grandma leaving in Dad and Mom's car to drive around and look at the crops. That left us kids home alone seeking opportunity for adventure. One of the things my three oldest siblings did during most of those visits was to take Grandpa and Grandma's car for a drive. At the time this started, Ron was 7, Janet was 8, and Caroline was 9 years old. Cars during those days were very roomy, especially Grandpa's 1947 Mercury. They would have to work together to make it work. One of them would be the driver, one would handle the accelerator and the other would handle the brakes. They would take turns at each job. Depending on the time they had, the ride was as short as driving around the windmill and as long as a mile and a quarter to our neighbor's and back. My sister Dianne, age 3, had the job of lookout at home. Also, she was to listen for me, as I was a baby at the time. The most important thing, my siblings told me, was to put the car back in the exact place Grandpa had parked it. They did this many times and were never caught. Many years later when Mom heard of these escapades, she could hardly believe it.

One of the important things about growing up on a farm was having to create your own fun. It taught us to be creative and industrious. It also taught us intrigue and planning.

My siblings and I learned to drive at an incredibly early age. I have a picture of me driving a tractor at age 5. The one memory I have from that time, was picking up bales of straw or hay in the field behind the granary. There were bales all over the field. We had a red Farmall tractor that pulled a big wooden sled behind it. My dad or my brother would put the tractor in gear for me, let out the clutch and hop off. My job was to drive next to each of the bales of hay or straw, so that my older brothers and sisters could stack them on the sled. When the sled was full, I would drive back to the barn. Ron or Dad would hop on the tractor and stop at the appropriate place. They would unload it and we would head back out into the field.

Another exciting time was when we were allowed to drive the cat. The cat was a powerful track driven type of tractor. It was not the Caterpillar brand, but we all called it the cat. What was neat about the cat was that it did not have a steering wheel! It had two levers with which to steer. If you wanted it to turn right, you pulled the right lever and if you wanted to go left you pulled the left lever. One of the important things when driving a cat was to not get it stuck. My brother, Ron, had done that one time and caught a lot of flak for it. The cat was used to pull other machinery out of the mud if they had gotten stuck. It becomes a big ordeal to get a cat unstuck. It was always a scary time when I was working on wet ground and would see the tracks slip a little. That always got your heart racing, causing you to be very attentive to your path. These are experiences I wish most kids could have. Experience is a great teacher.

CHAPTER 19
BIRTHDAY CAKES

I clearly remember my fifth birthday. The picture on the left is a snapshot of the birthday cakes on that day. In the picture (from right to left) are Grandpa Fontaine, Dad, Mom, Carolyn and then me. You can see the small birthday cake in front of me. The other cake was my brother Ron's. Our birthdays are three days apart and were often celebrated together. My cake had five candles and Ron's had thirteen. Ron and I sometimes shared a cake, and other times we would each have a big cake. This time was different. The day before this picture was taken, Mom made a big, beautiful cake for Ron and me to split. Mom had just finished frosting the cake when she turned around to take care of something on the stove. My brother John, who would turn 3 the following October, hopped up on the chair and started talking to Mom. During his conversation he decided to sit down on the table. Not knowing my cake was right behind him, he sat down and obliterated half of our cake. That is why my cake is shaped oddly. Mon baked another cake for Ron. I was not happy about what John had done. I was not there when it happened, but I bet Mom had a good laugh about it. Fortunately, there was enough cake for everyone to have their fill.

Baking cakes and pies was a daily chore at our house, especially during harvest season. My sister, Carolyn, made a lot of the sheet cakes and my sister, Jan, made most of the pies. Jan remembers baking five pies a day during those times. Mom made the birthday cakes. I loved watching her do her magic with her big wood handled frosting knife/spatula. It wasn't a knife, and it wasn't a spatula. It was rounded at the end and had a little flex to it. I'm sure there is a name for it.

The picture on the right was taken about seven weeks later, on July 27th, my dad's birthday. Mom made a special cake that looked like a shirt and tie. Dad was quite amazed by it. He wanted several pictures taken to commemorate the feat. As you can see in the picture, John was very taken by the cake also. It's great that Dad so thoroughly loved that birthday cake, as it was his last. He turned 40 that day and was gone a few months later. It makes me wonder if there is more than angel food cake in heaven. I know Dad really loved chocolate cake with butter on it. Knowing how much Dad loves the LORD, he probably can have chocolate cake with butter anytime he wants.

CHAPTER 20

DAD AND MOM ENTERTAINING

Mom and Dad loved entertaining. They would often have a large group of friends over for dinner and games. It was usually a group of 14 or 16 people. Each event was very lively and as a kid, fun to observe. Mom would go all out for these get-togethers. The good china, silverware and glassware would all be laid out exactly right. My older sisters and brother would help set up and serve. (That is my oldest sister, Carolyn, waving to the camera behind Dad.) The big drop leaf table with all the leaf inserts would fill the living room.

As guests arrived, they would put their coats on Mom and Dad's bed. Their bedroom was directly left of Carolyn in the picture. Left of the front of the picture was the den. The den had stairs that led up to our bedrooms and was also where the bar was set up. It was a joyful, noisy time.

My brother John and I, being about three and five years old when this picture was taken, were able to scurry around until dinner was served. We were always fed before the guests arrived. Once dinner was served, we were expected to be in our bedroom for the rest of the evening. After dinner, the dishes were cleared and different games, usually cards, would be played. Mom loved to tell the story about the time she brought out several games of "Cootie". She said the group had more fun that evening than ever before. The noise level in our farmhouse was significant.

One of the things that I loved doing after the guests had all arrived was to go into Mom and Dad's bedroom and smell the coats. They all had intriguing smells. The ladies' coats had different perfume smells and the men's coats were more like each other and had, what I would call today, a more professional smell. I remember there was always one of the men's coats that smelled like cherry pipe tobacco.

One of the frequent attendees was Joe Malone. Joe's nickname was "Champ". As youngsters, John and I only knew him as Champ. He was so memorable to us because he always gave John and me a dime when he saw us. Sometimes when Champ did not get to us before dinner, John and I would wait on the steps going up to our bedroom. Champ would always show up with two dimes for us and then, up we would go.

Our farmhouse had only one small bathroom. There was never a lock on the door because Mom said she needed to be able to pull my sisters out of the bathroom, especially on Sunday mornings before church, so that each of us could use it and not be late. Our church had two side balconies that Mom called "Horse Heaven". I can still hear her say, "Come on kids, we don't want to sit in Horse Heaven!"

A bathroom door without a lock was always tricky, especially during parties. If John or I had to use the bathroom during a party, we would have to sneak down and try to go unnoticed by Dad. I remember one time sneaking down successfully only to open the bathroom door, without knocking, to see one of the guests on the toilet. She was mortified. I had to hide in the kitchen until she was finished. I was sure she would not tell Mom or Dad what I had done. I remember wondering why she was so mortified. She had nine kids of her own and you would think that she would take something like this in stride. Anyway, I successfully made it back to the boys' bedroom and told my brother about the great adventure.

CHAPTER 21
1 BATHROOM / 7 KIDS

With six kids and one bathroom, there are a lot of stories around that room. As I have said previously, there was no lock on the door. Mom had to be able to move kids in and out of the bathroom in a timely manner and in the easiest fashion. Grandpa Fontaine put a lock on when we were gone somewhere. He or Grandma or both had been interrupted while they were in the bathroom by one of us kids. Mom promptly removed the lock after we got home. Also, she did not appreciate the holes in the woodwork from the lock. The door had a keyhole that you could see all the way through. The keyhole had been stuffed with cotton long before I arrived on the scene. The bathroom had a small sink and medicine cabinet on the left as you walked in. Then there was a tall metal cabinet that held towels, wash cloths and such. The toilet was in the left corner. The clawfoot bathtub took up most of the right side of the bathroom.

The bathroom was right off the kitchen. The kitchen was big and had a large table that we could all sit around. The kitchen table was where we spent most of our time. We ate at the table, played games, or just sat and talked. Over 90% of the visitors sat around the kitchen table after they arrived. Most extended family members just walked in without knocking and sat down. Each kitchen was like the town square of yesteryear. Mom told us a story about a time when Uncle Del came in and sat down at the kitchen table. He called out for Mom because she was not in the kitchen. She was in the bathroom and had walked in there, previously from her bedroom, not fully dressed. She said through the door, "Del, you are going to have to go outside and walk around for a minute and then come back in." Uncle Del laughed and as he went out the door he said, "Caught you with your pants down, eh!"

One of my earliest memories of that bathroom had to do with Dad. One day, Dad came rushing into the house and straight into the bathroom. I think I was the only one in the kitchen at the time. Less than a minute after Dad closed the door, I heard him say, "ACK!" Unbeknownst to him, Mom had painted the toilet seat shortly before Dad arrived. Mom came into the kitchen right about the time Dad said, "ACK". I remember Mom going into the bathroom. Through the closed door I could hear them talking and then Mom started to giggle and laugh. A brief time later she came out, closed the door, and got a can of turpentine and some rags. I could hear her chuckling the whole time she was in there cleaning up Dad.

Mom and my three sisters usually used the bathtub. My younger brother, John, and I usually bathed together until I was about five. It was then I felt brave enough to take a shower in the basement. In the summertime we boys had the whole outdoors when nature called. But in the winter, the girls had to time their baths appropriately. Another early memory involved my brother John and my sister Diane. Diane was taking a bath. John came in and needed to use the bathroom – now. Diane did not approve of John's request. John pleaded, stressing the urgency. Diane said it would be okay if he came in, but he had to keep his eyes on the ceiling. John agreed and entered the bathroom. A minute or two later we heard Diane yell out, "John! I said, "eyes on the ceiling!" That made all of us in the kitchen chuckle.

One of the highlights involving the bathroom was when Uncle Jim installed an exhaust fan in the wall. It made it a little less embarrassing when we had visitors hanging out in the kitchen. It also helped to dry the things that were hanging above the bathtub on a small clothesline. Mom and my sisters usually hung their dainty things on that line to dry. It was a little embarrassing for a little boy, but I got used to it. You can see that clothesline in the picture and Mom's fashionable winter morning wear.

CHAPTER 22
BABYSITTERS

Every year Dad and Mom would go away together for two weeks. They would hire a babysitter to come and stay with us kids. The babysitter did the cooking and cleaning. They did their best at directing us in the cleaning department. We had a couple of favorite babysitters. They had the honorary nickname of Grandma. There was Grandma Twite and Grandma Stroman. They were so nice. They were stereotypical Grandmas in that they were fluffy in size, gentle in spirit, good cooks, and ruled with kindness. We never wanted to hurt their feelings.

We had a couple of babysitters who were quite different. One, I remember, had a thing for spinach. She could have been Popeye's mother. It seemed like we had spinach at every meal.

In those days, spinach came in a can. I do not recall seeing it in any other form. Today's spinach comes fresh and is tasty. The canned spinach was neither. Most often the spinach was served in a vinegar base. Vinegar and kids taste buds are not a good match. We also had to eat what was on our plate. She served spinach in a soufflé, in a casserole, and in most of her hot dishes. Our muscles did not grow like Popeye's. It is funny; today I like spinach and especially when it is served in a vinegar base.

One babysitter, Mrs. "L," refused to take care of us again. We were too much of a handful for her. She was no Fraulein Maria as in "The Sound of Music." I remember several spankings from her. I know that it is hard to believe as I was such an angel. One night we were all sent to bed. At the top of the stairs, to the right was the girls' room and to the left the boys' room. On the landing, that night, was a full-size baby doll. The doll had rubbery type skin and a noisemaker that sounded like a cry when you would squeeze the doll. Ron and I took turns running to the landing and stepping on the doll. It would produce a cry that could be heard throughout the house, especially when Ron stepped on it. Ron was 12 years old at the time and I was 4. My stomp created a squeak and his, a long, loud cry. The babysitter was getting very annoyed with us. The doll stepping ended after Ron had stepped on it for about the fifth or sixth time. It was my turn. I ran to the landing to step on the doll and there was the babysitter waiting for me. I got a sound spanking and was sent back to bed. She took the doll with her. I remember Ron asking me what the spanking felt like. My response was, "It really burns!"

At a certain age, 10, 11, or 12, Ron and I could jump from those upstairs windows. It was a big jump, but Mom's flower bed was below. The ground was relatively soft and made it easy to roll forward onto the grass. One day, Ron was acting up, to the point of having Mrs. "L" come after him. He ran through the house with her chasing him. He ran up the stairs and around the corner into the boys' room. The upper left window you see in the picture was fully open. As Mrs. "L" came around the corner into the boys' room in pursuit of Ron, she saw him "tumble" out of the window. Of course, she screamed and then ran to the window. There was Ron, standing on the grass waving to her. That was the point of removal of all doubt on whether she would care for us again.

CHAPTER 23

COMBINES

Grain harvest is a busy time of year. Over the years, harvesting machines have changed dramatically. The picture on the top shows my mom and dad with their first equipment purchase. The harvesting machine in those days was a threshing machine. That is what Dad is pulling with the cat. Threshing was a high labor process. The grain had to be loaded by pitchfork into the threshing machine which separated the grain from the chaff. The power needed to run the threshing machine was provided by a tractor motor and a long belt that ran from the tractor to the threshing machine. The grain had to be bagged in gunnysacks as the process happened. Each gunnysack had to be sewn shut when it was filled, then loaded on a trailer. Farmers often worked together during threshing season, which helped cut down the labor costs.

The threshing machine evolved into a combine. A combine, like the picture on the left combined the power and the threshing into one machine. That is how the name originated. The combine that Dad purchased was a John Deere 65 pull type like the picture on the left. As you can imagine, much less labor is needed during harvest when using a combine.

One of my earliest memories about combining was when I was about four years old. Dad and all our neighbors had recently finished grain harvest. The exception was our neighbor, Howard Anderson, who lived a mile and a quarter from us. Howard was one of the last farmers in the area to have a dairy. It was exceedingly difficult to maintain a dairy and grow crops. Howard had one field left that needed to be combined. It was about 80 acres. The event that I remember happened because a big storm was approaching. Dad got on the phone and start calling all the other neighbors around us. Nearly all responded immediately. Howard's field was right across the highway from us. It was amazing to see tractors pulling combines being followed by trucks coming from every direction. When they all got there, I remember counting 14 combines and over 20 trucks in that field. Those 14 combines ate up that field in no time. It was all finished before the storm hit. It is interesting how events like that stick in your mind forever.

This next story involves the John Deere 65 again. This combine had three levers on the tongue where it attaches to the tractor. The levers were long so that the person on the tractor could reach them easily from the seat of the tractor. One lever was to put the combine into gear, another to raise and lower the pickup that put the grain windrow into the combine, and the third was to run the auger to empty the grain from the hopper into a truck. When running this type of combine you are constantly turning to the right watching the pickup and raising and lowering it as needed.

One day, my brother Ron was on the tractor with Dad while he was combining. Ron was about nine years old at the time. He asked Dad if he could go check the hopper, as he had done many times before, to see how full it was. Dad gave him the okay. As you can see in the picture, the ladder going up to the top of the hopper is right in front of the left wheel and tire. Ron hopped off the tractor and was about to climb the ladder when the tire caught his foot causing him to fall to the ground. Dad looked back to see the big combine tire about to run over Ron. By the time Dad stopped the tractor, the tire had rolled halfway up Ron's back. Dad had to back the combine up to get it off Ron. Fortunately, the ground was soft, and Ron came out of this unharmed. This really scared Dad. Mom said that when he carried Ron into the house, he was as white as a sheet and was crying. He had almost lost his oldest son that day. If Dad's hair were not already white, it would have turned white that day.

CHAPTER 24
ANDERSON'S PETS

The Anderson farm was a little over a mile from our farm. I loved to visit because it was the last working dairy in the area. Dad got rid of the dairy cows the year I was born. A working dairy was fun to see in action. Howard Anderson was the owner of the farm, and he had a brother named Sylvan who handled the dairy operation. It was fun to play in a hayloft that had hay in it. Once, I slid down the hay shoot because it looked like a fun slide. I hit the cement floor hard. I am surprised I did not break my tailbone. It took my breath away for a while; another lesson learned. Right across from that shoot was the bull pen. I always marveled at the bull's size and musculature. He was an intimidating looking animal. Most of my time was spent around Sylvan talking with him while he did his chores. He even let me ride on the tractor with him when he ran the manure spreader in the field. To me, that was an interesting and amusing piece of machinery. Boy, it could really fling the manure. Being around the barn most of the day, caused me to not mind the smell. It was amusing in that I would often visualize the mean kids at school standing behind the spreader when Sylvan would turn it on.

A couple of pets at the Andersons could be a challenge. The first problem pet was a goose. The path from their house to the barn required you to go over a small bridge that spanned a small creek. That is where the goose would hang out. I always had to be aware of where that goose was. If he saw you, he would attack just like what you see in the picture. Howard said to just give the goose a good kick and he would leave you alone. Well, that goose was half my size and was not about to give me even a second to think about kicking him. I do not know if you have ever been nipped by a goose, but it hurts. I wanted nothing to do with him. I was always ready to run when I got close to that bridge.

For a couple of years, they also had a horse. He was not a big horse. He was bigger than a pony but smaller than a full-size horse. That horse had a mean streak in him. The Andersons got rid of it because they could not break it of its meanness. I made the mistake one day of venturing out into the pasture, completely forgetting about the horse. I came out of the barn and noticed that all the cows were in a corner of the pasture. It looked like some of them were on the outside of the electric fence. Being curious, I walked out to them and found out that the electric fence was on the ground in that corner of the pasture. I headed back toward the barn to tell Sylvan about the fence. That is when I heard the horse coming up behind me. I looked back and saw him. His ears were flat against his head, meaning he was angry. I had one of those "Oh no!" moments. I took off running as fast as I could. I could tell by the sound of his hooves that he was gaining on me. I knew that I would not make it back to the barn in time to get away from him. Fortunately, Howard had installed four big poles in the pasture, in a straight line, about 50 feet from the barn. The poles were about 12 feet high and about 10 feet apart. The second and third pole had four, 2 x 6 boards attached to them, and those boards were about 2 feet apart from each other. It looked like a big ladder. The horse was inches behind me when I got to the first pole. I hooked my arm around the pole and swung around it. He went right past me and the pole and came to a skidding stop. It gave me just enough time to get to the second pole and start climbing to the top of that big "ladder". The horse was so mad that it charged at me as I climbed. He hit the bottom 2 x 6 so hard, he broke it. I cried out for help and, fortunately, Sylvan heard me. He came out and made the horse go away from the pole structure. That day I learned an important lesson on the dangers of absentmindedness.

The Andersons had a great dog named Rebel. He was smart, gentle, and enjoyed being around us. At milking time, most of the cows would be at the barn door waiting to come in. There were always one or two that wanted to stay out in the pasture. Sylvan would tell Rebel to get them. He would be off like a shot, round them up and get them into the barn. A treat that Mom would often have for us were caramel cubes. We loved those. We always saved one or two for Rebel. John or I would chew on the caramel to the point where it was soft and gooey. We would then give it to Rebel to finish off. It was hilarious to watch him. He loved the taste of those caramels, but being so gooey, the caramel would stick to the roof of his mouth. He would work at trying to get that caramel unstuck. His tongue and his drooling were working overtime. Occasionally, he would put his paw in his mouth which would cause him to get caramel on his paw. Rebel would eventually dissolve the caramel in his mouth and lick his paw clean. He always looked so satisfied when he finished.

CHAPTER 25

BEING AN ALTAR BOY

When I was in grade school, I was an altar boy. Whenever we were going to help serve mass, we had to put on the altar boy uniform. That included a cassock, which is the black inner garment in the picture, and a scapula which is the white outer garment. It was a cool job. One of the things I liked was lighting the candles on the altar. The tops of the candles were about 8 feet high. We used brass candle lighters that were about 6 feet long. At the top of the lighters, along with the waxed wick to light the candles, there was also a brass bell to snuff the candles after mass. We had to be careful not to get caught jousting or sword fighting with the candle lighters. That was a great temptation!

One of the cherished jobs was to be the altar boy on the right side of the altar. That is where the chimes were. The chimes were a grouping of six bells attached together that you got to ring at certain times during the mass. I loved that job. You had to get the timing exactly right or you were banned from the bells. At some point, before I stopped serving as an altar boy, the church switched to a single bell. That was not as enjoyable as the chimes. St. Anne's Church, another Catholic church in town, had a small three bar xylophone they used instead of bells. I thought that was cool, too.

Another interesting job was when you got to carry the censer. The altar boy in the picture is carrying one. A censer is what is used to burn incense at certain times during a high mass. Inside the censer there was a disk about the size of a Peppermint Patty. Before the mass, we would light that disk and it would burn like a charcoal briquette, but much slower. The priest would put incense on that disk once or twice during the mass. Of course, that meant there was a lot of incense smoke coming out of the censer. If he put on a lot of incense, the rising smoke could make your nose hurt and your eyes water while you were standing holding the censer. I remember, at times, trying to inconspicuously blow the smoke away with my mouth.

Usually the priest used the censer, but sometimes the altar boy also used it. Holding the top of the chains with your left hand you would pick it up by the chain about three quarters of the way down. Then you would swing it to get incense smoke everywhere. You would only swing it three times at each stop. Each time you swung the censer it would hit the chains that hung down between your left hand and right hand. I always liked the sound it made when hitting the chains. There was always a lot more action with the censer when the bishop was there. At those times, the incense smell could really fill the church. Incense can come in many different fragrances. Some smell good and some do not. My Grandpa Fontaine, who attended St. Anne's, did not like the incense the church had recently purchased, so he offered to change their incense. He bought them a whole year's supply!

Another thing we had to be careful not to get caught doing, was sipping on the left-over wine in the cruets. That was rare but always a tasty treat. Being an altar boy helped me to tone down my shenanigans. I had an image to live up to and at times I was able to do that. I wish more boys could have the experience of being an altar boy.

CHAPTER 26

CLIMBING TREES

We had a lot of trees around the farmhouse. About every homestead had a grove of trees around it. This provided protection from winter storms. In the summertime, I loved to climb the big cottonwood trees that were closest to the house. They were huge. There was one that I climbed most often. It was right on the edge of the yard and about 50 feet from the back door. This tree had its first large branch close enough for a seven or eight-year-old to jump up, grab, and swing up onto it. That tree had to be at least 60 feet high, and it tested my fear factor the higher I would climb. It was great exercise and taught me how to focus. There have been studies done about the benefit of climbing trees.

According to a press release from UNF (University of North Florida), the results demonstrated remarkable cognitive gains: "After two hours, participants were tested again, and researchers found that their working memory capacity had increased by 50 percent, a dramatic improvement."

I remember falling only twice. Once was before my seventh or eighth birthday, where I fell about 15 feet to the ground. I sprained my wrist and ankle. It is the only birthday I remember being hurt.

The second fall happened when I was quite a way up in the tree. This one was the most memorable. I was out on a limb, like the boy in the picture. I lost my footing and started to fall. I tried to grab the limb with my arms but was not able to prevent the fall. I fell maybe 5 feet, even though it felt like 15 feet, to the next branch below me. I was able to catch that branch and hold on. I remember looking down and seeing how far I was from the ground. I probably would have broken something had I not caught that limb.

Our youngest daughter, Christina, also loved to climb trees. Many times, she would bring a book along. She would find a comfortable spot in our big apple tree and settle down for an hour or two of reading. One day, early on in her climbing adventures, we heard her cry out. She had slipped and would have fallen out of the tree had it not been for her pink Oshkosh B'gosh shortalls catching on a stub of a branch. The heavy-duty fabric of those shortalls kept her dangling in the tree until she could be rescued. I am glad it did not stop her from climbing trees.

CHAPTER 27

EXPLODING STOVE

Propane fed gas stoves were a necessity where I grew up. In winter, it was not unusual to lose electrical power for days at a time. Our only heat source became the kitchen stove. Fortunately, our kitchen was large and could accommodate the whole family. We had a big kitchen table that we could all sit around. Our gas stove was like the ones in the pictures. The second picture reminds me of those days. We would have coats on, oven door open, and the stovetop in use. Without electrical power, we did not have water either. We would have to go and get buckets of snow to melt on the stovetop. Having a bucket of water from melted snow in the bathroom was important. That bucket provided the water to flush the toilet. With all of us kids, we were constantly melting snow.

Our bedrooms were upstairs, and I remember waking up on those powerless mornings being able to see my breath. I did not want to get out of bed because I was warm under the covers. But soon nature would call, and I could also smell breakfast cooking. I would dash out of bed, get dressed, and head to the kitchen. We boys were encouraged to use the outdoors rather than the bathroom when appropriate. That cut down on melting more snow.

Mom loved cooking with gas. In fact, when something was going right, Mom would often say, "Now we are cooking with gas!" Cooking with gas was much different than using an electric stove. You had to understand the properties of gas and the importance of lighting the burner as soon as you turned on the gas. We had a wooden match dispenser on the wall beside the oven. We would always light the match first and then turn on the oven, broiler, or burner. If, for some reason, the match went out before lighting one of those three things, you always turned off the gas before grabbing another match. We all grew up understanding these rules.

There were two ways to light the oven. One way was to open the oven door, look for the hole on the bottom of the oven in the front. You would light your match, turn on the gas, and put the match through that hole. Sometimes it worked, sometimes it did not. The second way was to open the broiler door at the bottom of the oven, light your match, holding it with your first two fingers, turn on the gas, and reach in and hold the match up by the broiler. That always worked unless you dropped the match. We usually lit the oven the second way.

When Mom remarried and she and my stepdad, Lee, were on their honeymoon, Grandma Fontaine was staying out at the farm while they were away. Grandma was not familiar with the gas oven. One afternoon she called my sister, Diane, to help her light the oven. Grandma was not having any success. My guess is that she tried the first way by lighting the oven through the hole in the oven. That method had a lower success rate because the match would often go out before the gas got to it. Diane said, "Okay Grandma!" Diane went through the routine of lighting the stove from below. She did not know about Grandma's repeated attempts to light the stove the other way. There was quite a buildup of gas that ignited as soon as Diane reached in with the match. It was an explosion that shook the house. It threw Diane clear across the kitchen and against the sink. We all rushed to the kitchen. We saw Diane sitting on the floor against the sink crying, "My hair! My hair!" The explosion burned her bangs and eyebrows off. It mangled her two fingers that were holding the match. We made sure Diane was okay and that she was not smoking anywhere and got her fingers bandaged up. There was one thing that made us laugh. Grandma's nylons had huge holes in them from the explosion. She kept looking at them and saying, "My lands!"

Before I wrote this, I called Diane to make sure my facts were right. There were two things that I had forgotten. The first was, Diane had a special school dance coming up the next weekend and she still went without bangs or eyebrows. I really laughed when she told me the second thing. She said, "You would think the explosion would also burn off my mustache! But Noooo!"

I love talking to my siblings to confirm the facts of the stories they were involved in. I learn something new with each phone call. The expected 15- or 20-minute call, to confirm the facts, has always turned into a 1 to 2-hour reminiscing time. I was hoping I was not being a pest by calling to confirm details. Each have said, "No! Call any time. We love talking about the stories." Each call brings such added joy to the stories.

CHAPTER 28

FRIGHTENING MOVIES

 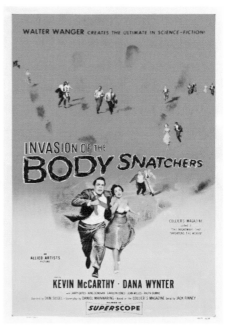

The first scary movie I saw on the big screen, as a kid, was "The Blob," starring Steve McQueen. I was seven years old when my brothers and sisters and I attended the movie. The movie kept getting scarier and scarier. The Blob came from outer space and was about the size of a softball when it was discovered. Of course, it was first discovered by a farmer. He picked it up with a stick and it started to come down the stick to his arm. It is attached to his arm and that is when Steve McQueen and his girlfriend show up and see this farmer in agony. They load him into the car and take him to the doctor. In the doctor's office you see the sheet that is over the man start to get bigger and bigger. You never saw what was happening under the sheet, but you knew it was not good.

The Blob grew as it consumed the unsuspecting extras in the movie. One of the scariest parts of the movie was when The Blob gets into the projector room in the Colonial movie theater. After he gets the projectionist, The Blob starts to ooze out the openings in the back of the theater where the projector was. Well, that caused all of us to turn around and look at those openings in our own theater. Oh good, it was not happening here…yet. Anyway, they end up containing The Blob and moving it to the North Pole. Talk about worries with global warming. I remember going to bed that night. I had to thoroughly check under my bed to make sure there was no red blob that might get me.

The second scary movie I watched on the big screen was, "Invasion of the Body Snatchers." Well, it was the third movie. That night there was a double feature. The first movie was pretty low-budget and not very scary. German Shepherd dogs helped take out the aliens, so, I thought that was cool. But the second movie was "Body Snatchers." That was a very suspenseful movie with very few special effects. You did not know who you could trust. It was cloning way before its time. The aliens looked just like your neighbors because they were clones of your neighbors and controlled by an alien mindset. I do not think we saw what the aliens initially looked like. The key was to never fall asleep, or they would get you.

One of the big advantages of earlier movies like these was the building suspense. Today's movies jump right in with overwhelming special effects and little suspense. Back then, you built much better special effects in your mind than what they could create on the screen. I will take an old-time scary movie over today's horror movies every time. Give me a good old Boris Karloff, Lon Chaney, Jr. or Bela Lugosi movie and I will be happy.

CHAPTER 29
JOHN AND GRANDPA FONTAINE

Grandpa Fontaine and brother John had some funny interactions. Grandpa Fontaine did not think they were so funny at the time. Grandpa liked to sharpen anything that needed sharpening. He had a red handled hatchet. I have it hanging in my garage now and every time I see it, I think of the time when

John was four years old and got ahold of Grandpa's hatchet. Grandpa came out and saw John sitting on the ground happily chopping a brick. Grandpa's voice had a French nasal tone that was accentuated by a lot of air. When he was upset each word sounded like it came from the bottom of his lungs. Seeing John hitting a brick with his newly sharpened hatchet, Grandpa said, "Chohnny, what—are—you-- doing!" Grandpa took the hatchet away from John and John just looked up with his big brown eyes and said, "Grandpa, I was just axing!" John got a good scolding. When Grandpa scolded, he would hold up his right index finger. You could not miss it. His fingers were twice as thick as a normal man's. So, we paid close attention.

We loved combing Grandpa's hair. When he was out at the farm he usually sat on the end of the sofa. As kids, we would sit on the arm of the sofa and comb Grandpa's hair. He would hand us his comb, which was the signal that it was okay to start combing. One of the times when John was combing Grandpa's hair, he unexpectedly stopped combing, walked outside, and threw Grandpa's comb onto the roof of the house. John had gotten a scolding earlier that day from Grandpa and remembered it during the combing session. John came back into the house empty-handed. Grandpa wanted to know where his comb was. John took him outside and pointed to the comb on the roof. "Chohnny" got another scolding. After Grandpa finished scolding, John said, "You better watch out, Grandpa. I won't let you come to my house anymore."

Even as a little boy, John could imitate Grandpa very well. We would all laugh heartily when he broke out into his Grandpa Fontaine routine. Grandpa had a distinctive walk that John had down perfectly. He also had Grandpa's forceful voice down pat. If there was a rug that was out of place or had a corner turned up, Grandpa always used his feet to fix it. It was humorous to watch Grandpa do it, but it was hilarious to watch John imitate him. Grandpa also had a unique way to kill flies with the flyswatter. When he saw a fly in the house, he would get the flyswatter and go after the fly. Grandpa would hit that fly with five times the force needed to do the job. If the fly fell dead to the windowsill, he would forcefully smack it once or twice again. Then he would push it off the windowsill and onto the floor where he would proceed to step on it. The fly was not just dead, it was certainly dead. The fly swatting was always a part of John's imitation. At Grandpa's funeral, John went into his routine. He had everyone who had spent considerable time with Grandpa laughing out loud. Grandma Fontaine so enjoyed John's imitation that day. In many ways, John and Grandpa were two peas in a pod. Of all of us kids, John is the one who most resembles Grandpa and keeps him fresh in our minds.

CHAPTER 30
FARM "MISHAPS"

Whenever we had family get-togethers, many of the stories you have read would be retold and relived each night. The only thing missing was a good night's sleep. Most nights we talked and laughed until the break of dawn. My brother-in-law, Brad, would go to bed at a normal time and get a good night's sleep. He was the only one. My sister-in-law, Jeannie, would often make it to about midnight. She would head off to bed and then we would see her again about 15 to 30 minutes later. She would always return saying, "I don't want to miss anything!" Mom would sit in a comfortable chair and doze between loud bouts of laughter. We would say, "Mother dear, please go to bed." She would say, "No, I want to be here."

Other than Mom, you did not want to fall asleep in the same room as the rest of us. There was a strong possibility that you would get shaving cream put in your relaxed hands and then get your nose tickled with a feather. We did that with Brad. We had forgotten that he scratched his nose with his wrist rather than the palm of his hand. That turned out to be even funnier. We kept tickling his nose to no avail. Our sister, Jan, finally stepped in and woke Brad up and helped him up to bed. Brad went straight to bed when he was tired from that time on.

We all had stories to go with each scar. John would show us the scar he had on the top of his head and tell the story. The Hanson boys were over one day. They had discovered, on their farm, you could release the stop on the crank on the grain elevator/auger. The grain elevator would come down quickly and the crank would spin like crazy. Well, there was a cranked-up grain elevator (like the one in the picture) in our yard that day. We went over to it and John released the stop. Everything worked as expected except the realization that the spinning crank handle got lower as the elevator was coming down. John was in the way when the handle reached his height. He was knocked to the ground and had a nice gash on his scalp. Well, that put a damper on the afternoon's fun. Mom got him all patched up.

We all had comparable stories to tell and laugh about. You have read several of mine. It would take several sleepless nights to get to them all. We would talk about rock fights, firecracker wars, falling out of trees, wounded visiting cousins from the city, and so many more stories.

There were stories of injuries and close calls, but the stories about Mercurochrome would make us all wince and laugh. With that stuff there were times when we wondered which was worse, the injury or the cure. When Mercurochrome was applied, even to a small cut, it would burn like crazy. One time, my cousin was visiting from California. We were the same age, and he was staying out at the farm. One day, as we were running through some big cement culverts, he did not keep his head down low enough. The top of his scalp got scraped by a piece of cement. The injury to his scalp caused him to fall forward and scrape up his knee. Off to Mom we went. Mom cleaned up the scrapes and started to apply the Mercurochrome to the scrape on the top of his head. It was his first experience with Mercurochrome. I had never heard a boy scream so loudly as he did. It took a lot of talking from Mom to allow her to apply the dreaded substance to the scrape on his knee. There was another bloodcurdling scream with him saying that his knee was on fire. If you have ever had Mercurochrome applied to a cut or scrape, you know what he was feeling. We were happy when Mom switched from Mercurochrome to iodine.

CHAPTER 31

CONFISCATED
BIRTHDAY PRESENTS

My birthday is in early June. It is a fun time to have a birthday. It is the beginning of summer, school's out and fun times are ahead. Whatever I got as a gift for my birthday was something I could enjoy all summer long. A couple of birthday gifts I received as a boy did not stay in my possession for very long. One of those gifts was a BB gun. It was such a cool BB gun. It was something I really wanted and was overjoyed when I received it. I was given a couple of paper targets and a bunch of BBs to practice with. I became a good shot very quickly. One day, I was presented with a target that caught my attention. My brother was across the yard and bending over. We were both husky fellows and both wore blue jeans. I knew the BB would not penetrate the blue jeans as he was far enough away. It would only sting in a padded part. What I failed to do was begin with the right end in mind. Had I thought it through, he would have yelped, run after me, failed to catch me, and then would go tell Mom. I did not begin with the right end in mind. The end was, go tell Mom. Everything happened as described. Mom confiscated my BB gun and I never saw it again. Pleading, promises, and commitment to extra chores had no effect. To this day I have no idea what Mom did with that BB gun.

The second birthday gift that was confiscated from me was a set of walkie-talkies. They were cool walkie-talkies. The sound was clear, they were lightweight, and a camo green color. This is another story of not thinking things through.

Every summer we had a Hispanic family who worked on our farm, thinning and hoeing sugar beets. The head of the family was Henry Laura. He and his wife had six kids. The oldest was Tony, who drove a beautiful 1956 red Thunderbird with a continental kit on the back. The next to oldest were daughters named China and Maria. Maria was beautiful and I had a crush on her. The next was a son named Johnny, who was my age. Next came Lily and then Valdo. Some Hispanics have difficulty pronouncing the letter "V". It sounds like the letter "B". So, Valdo was always called Baldo. Lily and Baldo were closer to my brother's age. We all played nonstop while they were with us. The house they stayed in was more of a cabin and was only used for about six weeks every summer. It did not have indoor plumbing, which meant there was an outhouse. It was a two-seater like the one in the picture and was about 40 or 50 feet from the back door of the house. It was on the edge of the grove of trees that separated our homes. I came up with the bright idea to utilize my walkie-talkies in a fun way. I was nine or 10 years old at the time. I decided to hide one of the walkie-talkies in the outhouse. I hid in the grove of trees and waited for one of the girls to use the outhouse. After a short wait, China came out and used the outhouse. I gave her a chance to sit down and then over my walkie-talkie I broadcasted, "Hey, hey, I'm painting down here!" Well, there were a lot of Spanish words that I did not understand and then China came racing out of the outhouse and into the house. She brought her dad out to investigate. They did not find my walkie-talkie. I remember Henry using the word "loco" a couple of times when he was talking to China. I should have retrieved my walkie-talkie at that point. But it was so funny to see what happened, I decided to risk another event. After a while, Maria came out to use the outhouse. I hesitated due to the crush I had on her. But hoping for a funny result caused me to do it again. The result was the same, except this time Henry found my walkie-talkie. He took it over to our home and handed it to my mother explaining what I had done. I had to profusely apologize to Henry. My walkie-talkies were never seen again.

CHAPTER 32
MINNESOTA SNOW

Growing up in northern Minnesota meant that there was snow in the wintertime. Sometimes a lot of snow and other times an unbelievable amount of snow. The biggest snowdrift that I experienced as a kid turned out to be 25 feet high and it was right behind our house. It was as high as the upstairs windows. The picture on the left was one of those times when my dad was younger. He is standing on a snowbank with our neighbor. When we had that big drift behind our house, we were able to dig into it at its base and create a room inside. It was cool to sit inside. I remember wishing I had a girlfriend to help keep me warm. I think I was in second grade at the time.

We could see the entrance to that room from the window in the den. I remember having a nightmare one night that involved that room. Aliens had taken it over! In my dream you knew they were in there because you could see eerie flashing lights and feel a distinct sense of fear. That nightmare startled me awake. I finally convinced myself to go down into the den and make sure everything was okay in our snowbank room. I remember turning on the den light and instantly seeing a light in the snow room. It took my breath away for a couple seconds until I realized it was the den light shining into it. Some scary movies I had watched had gotten the best of me that night.

"It's snowing so hard you can't see the barn!" That always brought anyone within earshot to the picture window to see the snowfall. The picture on the right gives you the view we had from that window. After the barn was torn down, we could still get Mom to rush to the window when we say, "It's snowing so hard you can't see the barn!" After rushing to the window, Mom would look at us and then say, "Oh, you ninny."

At the end of our driveway, you could turn right to go to the highway or left to take the gravel road into town. Across the road from that intersection, Uncle Del, my dad's brother, built a Quonset and two grain bins. After a snowstorm there was always a good-sized snowdrift crossing the road on each side of our driveway. If the snowdrifts were less than 3 feet high, I was the one who had to try my best to break through the drift on the right that led to the highway. I had a 55 Chevy and 58 Chevy during those years. They had a lot of metal to them. I would back up to the drift on the left which was about 100 feet from the drift on the right. I would then race forward and try to break through the drift. Sometimes it took several tries to make it all the way through. Other times we had to wait for the snowplows to come through to get out of our driveway. When we knew a significant storm was approaching, we would park the car on the road a little past where the drift was going to be. We had a several hundred-foot extension cord that we would run from the house to the car. We would plug that cord into the head bolt heater on the engine. It was needed if you wanted to start your car on a very wintry morning. Without plugging it in, you would turn the key and hear, RRRR...rrrr...r. Then nothing. That was no fun when it was 30 below zero. People visiting from warmer states would often ask what the plug sticking out of the front of your car was for. Sometimes you could get away with telling them that it was an electric car. Come to think of it, I had an almost Tesla.

CHAPTER 33

MINNESOTA STATE FAIR

Growing up in northern Minnesota, one of the highlights for the year was attending the Minnesota State Fair. As a kid, it was a place of wonder and joy. There were so many people and so many things to see. The first stop, once inside the gate, was the Tom Thumb Donuts stand. Those (warm little cinnamon sugar covered donuts) were amazing. I remember my mouth watering as we got close to the entry gates. As far as I knew, the fair was the only place in the entire world to get those little donuts. The first bite would cause you to close your eyes and savor every flavor. My earliest memory of the cost was $.25 a bag. What a deal.

Also, in those days, you could go on all the fair rides for about five dollars. The Tilt-a-Whirl, Scrambler, Spider, Roller Coaster, Bumper Cars, and Ferris Wheel were my favorite rides. Mom was such a trooper. She loved going on the rides with us.

Even in later years, Mom never missed a chance to go on a scary ride with our kids. I can hear her laugh now. I also love amusement park rides. The scarier the better. One year, Mom came out to visit during our Rose Festival. The last picture is of Mom and my daughter, Jennie, on a small but crazy roller coaster. Also, there was a new ride that year. I do not remember what it was called, but four people sat inside a rocket shaped module. The whole module was aluminum bars. The only solid metal was the floor which had four seatbelts. The ride was a cross between the Spider and a roller coaster. I had my doubts about Mom, our girls, and me going on this wild ride. It was a wild ride that tickled you from the inside out. I had never heard Mom laugh so hard in all my life.

The sideshows at the fair were always so amazing. You could see the Sword Swallower, the Bearded Lady, the Fat Man, the Tall Man, the Tiny Man, the Electric Chair in action, the Woman with Two Heads (that was a little cheesy), and so many more oddities.

It was also fun to watch people trying to win a prize at all the different games. I figured out early on that those games were rigged. I do remember winning a foot-long cigar that was almost 2 inches in diameter. I tried lighting it when I got home and found it was filled with sawdust. One year my sister, Carolyn, and her boyfriend, Charlie, went to the fair with us. Charlie was a semi-pro, fast pitch softball pitcher. One of the games available was one where you try to knock down three pewter bottles with a softball. Charlie knew that one of the bottles usually weighed 8 to 10 pounds. By how the gamekeeper handled the bottles, you could tell which one was the heaviest. Charlie would wind up and nail that bottle each time. He won the big prize for my sister and was not allowed to play again.

The last time I attended the Minnesota State Fair was when I was 19 years old. Racing was the reason I was there. The fair held the biggest race of the year. Racers came from all over the country. I was part of a pit crew of one of the top racing teams in the five-state area. We ran a Sprint car. Wyman Wade, #39, was the owner and driver. He was an amazing driver to observe. What I liked about the fair that year was I was able to wear the team uniform around the fairgrounds all weekend. It was so much easier to talk to pretty girls while wearing my racing outfit. I look forward to going back to the fair sometime soon. And, of course, my first stop will be to get Tom Thumb donuts.

CHAPTER 34
UNCLE JIM

Have you ever had someone in your life who seemed larger than life? This was Uncle Jim (pictured). He was my mom's brother. He was that person in our family's lives. Uncle Jim was the head electrician for Aramco (Arabian American Oil Company). He knew King Saud personally. Every 18 months, Aramco gave Uncle Jim an all-expense paid vacation. He traveled the world, and about every five years, he would come home to Crookston, Minnesota. He often had movies of some of his latest exploits.

For example, he was the first person, on record, to ride a motorcycle across the Sahara Desert lengthwise. The Arabs did not like that he used a Triumph motorcycle because it was English made. They did not like the English then. That occurred when my older siblings were in high school. He was invited to the high school to show his documentary movie to all the students. Another time when he was home, he showed us a documentary of a waterskiing exhibition he did for the King. That also was very cool. Uncle Jim was an amazing water skier, including skiing off big jumps built in the water. He received many watches from King Saud, but the one he received after the skiing exhibition was unbelievable. He showed us the watch, I don't remember the brand, but it had a diamond embedded at each numeral and on the outside of the watch there were two full circle rows of black diamonds then two more circles of white diamonds! It was awesome to see. When he came during the summer it was always great to go to the lake and watch him ski.

Uncle Jim had exceptional stories about all the faraway countries he traveled to. He was also an excellent pilot. When he would come home, he would rent a plane and fly himself and his family into town. It was exciting to go out to our little airport and see him land the plane and pull up to where we were. One of the times when he came home, I was 17 years old. It was during harvest time, and I was combining wheat. Uncle Jim and family were coming over for dinner that evening, and I was so looking forward to it. Unbeknownst to me, he and his wife flew to Hillsboro, North Dakota to pick up my girlfriend to join us. He buzzed the field where I was combining. My girlfriend, Deanna, got a little green around the gills when he did that. He would land right at the farm and come right into the yard. He seemed larger than life! I had to laugh when I heard last summer from someone who knows Deanna now, that she does not remember me, but she remembered Uncle Jim and the plane!

Uncle Jim always had several magic tricks he would show us. We loved him because he took time to spend with all of us kids. He would go roller skating with the older kids, which he was expert at. My sisters loved going dancing with him because he knew all the latest dances. I think the focused time he spent with us was what made him so special.

I feel so fortunate that our daughters have three bigger than life uncles in their lives. The focused attention that my brothers gave our daughters makes them bigger than life too.

CHAPTER 35
UNCLE LOUIE

I had several uncles named Louie growing up. This story is about Uncle Louie on my Grandma Fontaine's side. Uncle Louie was married to Grandma's sister, Lillian. Whenever they would come to visit, my mom would host a dinner. There were always several relatives who attended the dinner. With this size of group, we always had dinner in the living room. We had a large, drop-leaf dining room table with four additional leaf inserts that would extend the table out about 12 feet. At the far end of the table was another table that sat four or six people. That was usually the kid's table. Uncle Louie most often sat at the end of the big table right next to the kid's table.

The relatives on Mom's side of the family tended to be slow eaters. When my brothers and sisters and I would sit down to eat, it was not a slow eating process. We could all put away a lot of food in a short period of time. So, to try and slow our eating down at big dinners with slow eaters, we had to provide some entertainment between bites. Grandpa Fontaine always had his dessert with the main meal. He was the only one that did that. I remember counting the number of forkfuls of the main course he would take before taking a bite of dessert. He was consistent and slow, which got boring after a few minutes. It was a bit of a two-edged sword to do that. It passed the time, but we could see what the dessert was and knew we would not be getting any until all the slow eaters were finished with the main meal. Other slow eaters would chew each bite over 20 times before swallowing. Mom thought we were listening intently to the adult conversation, but we were counting chews.

Grandma Fontaine could be a bit of a prankster at times like this. Occasionally she would bring a box of chocolates and put them on a silver platter. All the chocolates were the same color and size with different fillings in each. She had one fake chocolate that was made of rubber. At the end of the meal, she would hand the platter around and wait to see who got the rubber chocolate. She got the biggest kick out of that. She would laugh so hard it would bring a tear or two to her eyes. She would always reach in her sleeve and get the tissue that was always there to dab her eyes. We all loved her laugh.

Grandpa and Uncle Louie usually had a couple of stiff drinks before dinner. You could say they enjoyed "bending an elbow" together when Uncle Louie and Aunt Lillian came to visit. So, Uncle Louie was usually in a good mood by dinnertime. One of the things we learned about Uncle Louie was that he was very polite when asked to pass something around the table. He was so polite that even if he were about to take a bite of food, he would set his fork down and pass whatever was asked for. So, the kids table came up with a game called "Who can get the food closest to Uncle Louie's mouth." We did not want to be too obvious. He would put food on his fork and start moving towards his mouth. One of us would then say, "Uncle Louie, would you please pass the salt," or something close to him. He would always stop mid-bite, put his fork down and hand us what we asked for. We would allow him to get a bite or two in and then the next one of us kids would have a chance at how close we could get the fork to Uncle Louie's mouth. We had to stifle our snickers and snorts so as not to alert Mom to our little game. When we could not contain our joy, Mom would give us "the look". That ended the game. I do not think we ever made it to dessert time with Uncle Louie before being shut down by "the look". The Uncle Louie story is always relived when our family gets together.

CHAPTER 36
GRANDMA FONTAINE'S HUMOR

Grandma Fontaine's humor always tickled us. It was so much fun to see her unable to control her laughter. Her whole body would shake, and tears would be caught by the Kleenex tissue she always had up her sleeve. We never knew what would set her off.

One day she got a call from her next-door neighbor, Desta Smith. She and her husband were quite elderly. Mrs. Smith called and was extremely worried about what her husband had just done. Grandma, in a concerned tone, asked Mrs. Smith what the problem was. Mrs. Smith told her that her husband had just brushed his teeth with Brylcreem. He had gotten the tubes mixed up. As best she could, Grandma calmed Mrs. Smith's fear. She said he would be all right, and to just rinse his mouth very well. As soon as Grandma hung up the phone she started to laugh, shake, and tear up at the situation. It always took a fair amount of time before Grandma would return to normal. It was so much fun to observe.

Another time was when Mom and Grandma were at the drugstore together. A local woman walked in after just having her hair done at Merle Norman's Hair Salon. All this woman's hair was piled on top of her head in a Bouffant/Beehive hairdo. Grandma took one look and started to giggle and shake. She had to hurry out of the drugstore so she could allow the rest of her laugh to escape. Mom stayed inside and complemented the woman on her new hairdo. I think she would have loved to have been outside laughing with Grandma.

A lot of local theater happened in Crookston when I was little. My Dad participated in a couple of plays. Grandma and Mom enjoyed going to those plays together. At one play they were enjoying, a new character came on stage. He was an elderly man who walked slowly and was a little bowlegged. Grandma had to get up and leave immediately. Mom followed her out wondering what was wrong. When they were in the lobby, Grandma did her usual laughing routine. Grandma got out, between her giggles and laughs, that the actor that came on stage looked like he was "carrying a load in his pants". I would have loved to see those two laughing themselves to tears in the lobby.

Another time, Grandma, again lost it in the theater. The play was over, and everyone was exiting the theater. Grandma and Mom were in the balcony this time. As they came down the stairs, Grandma was holding the wide wooden railing and talking with Mom. Unbeknownst to Grandma, there was a truly short, bald man at the base of the stairs and in-line with the railing. Grandma, being distracted by talking to Mom, put her hand on top of this man's head, thinking it was part of the railing. Of course, he jumped aside, startling Grandma, wondering what she was doing. That was another time they had to exit quickly before they burst with laughter.

When I was a teenager, Grandma came out to the farm and was laughing from the moment she got out of the car. She had a hard time telling the story through her laughter. She had just stopped for gas at the gas station in town. She happened to look over at a man who had just gotten out of his car on the other side of the pumps. She said he had a shiny bald head. As soon as she noticed how shiny his head was, a big bird flew over and dropped a big "bomb" on the forward part of his scalp. The dropping proceeded down this man's forehead and then down his nose. I don't know which was funnier, the story or watching Grandma tell it. I surely miss her.

CHAPTER 37
7TH AND 8ᵀᴴ GRADES

Seventh and eighth grades at Cathedral Grade School bring back many memories. Most of the good memories had to do with sports. The classroom memories were not as good. The nuns decided to separate the boys from the girls for the last two years of grade school. It may have been because Cathedral High School had gone to an all-boys school. They were preparing us for that eventuality. I do not think that was a particularly clever idea. Having girls in the class helped calm down the boy's rowdiness. With no girls in class, the rowdiness escalated. We had the same Nun, Sister Ida, for both seventh and eighth grade. She was an older nun who had taught my dad. She was nice until you significantly "ticked her off". She was a believer in corporal punishment. Her two main implements were a large chalkboard eraser and the traditional rubber tipped wooden pointer. The chalkboard eraser was about 12 inches long and relatively soft, top, and bottom. It never really hurt when she would hit us with it. If she were angry, she would whack us three or four times about the head and shoulders. Again, it really did not hurt, you just could not breathe for a while due to the chalk in the air around your head. We also had to work on getting all the chalk from our clothes before we went home. That was a telltale sign that we had acted up in school. Now the pointer had some sting to it and could leave a welt on your arm. If you got her really upset, she could turn you into a three striped sergeant very quickly. There were a few of us who earned quite a few stripes over those two years. Sister Ida had two favorite sayings, "Oh joy" and "Gash". Those were her swear words. In those days men and women who did not swear had their own non-swear words. Mom often uses the word "Cripes" or "For cripes sake". Dad did not allow any swearing from the hired men. One day I heard one of our hired men, Leo Page, say several times while he was working on some machinery, "Oh CPR". I thought it was a swear word that I had not heard before and told my dad that Leo was swearing. My Dad went out and talked to Leo and returned chuckling. He told me that CPR meant Canadian Pacific Railroad and that he was not really swearing.

Sister Ida, as I mentioned, taught my dad, and knew how involved he was at the church. She thought the world of him. When I would act up, she would say, "Why can't you be more like your father?" That would always straighten me out for a while. Sister Ida was easy to talk with and occasionally she would get a question that would throw her for a loop. My best friend, Greg, had heard an unfamiliar word and asked Sister Ida, "Sister, what is a prostitute?" She stuttered and stammered over that question and ended up telling Greg to ask his parents.

Cathedral High School's athletic teams were called the "Blue Wave". The grade school athletic teams were called the "Ripples", continuing the water theme. Our cheerleaders mimicked an advertising jingle for Nestlé's chocolate. "N E S T L E S, makes the very best chocolate." The jingle elongated the word chocolate at the end. Our cheerleaders would sing, "R I P P L E S, Ripples makes the very best touchdown!" (Elongate touchdown). I loved playing football. I was the fullback and co-captain of the team. Fr. Storr was our coach and was not well suited for the job. He had a quick temper and used language not fitting a priest. But we had fun.

Hockey is what I enjoyed the most. I was one of the biggest kids in grade school and was quite fast on the ice. If a breakaway happened by the other team, meaning one of the players was heading toward our goal alone, I was generally able to overtake him and get the puck away from him. One day, we were playing a team where that happened three times. One of their players usually hung back behind all the rest of us while we were shooting on their goal. Three times one of their players got the puck and passed it to him. Each time, when he would take off toward our goal, I would come up from behind him and steal the puck. The third time I did that to him, he was so angry he hit me in the face with the butt of his stick. He broke my nose. Had it not been for the bleeding, I believe I would have torn him apart. Much of my adult career required that I call on plastic surgeons and ENTs. Many of them would look at me from across the desk and say they could fix that for me if I wanted to. My reply always was, "No thanks. I have all my teeth, and this is the only evidence I played hockey."

In seventh grade our team, Noah's Knights, won the city championship. It was a great game. We won 1 – 0. The following year, when I was captain of the team, we also took top honors. I will never forget that final game. I was in the zone, scoring a hat trick, meaning I scored three goals. I scored the last two goals within nine seconds of each other. Tony Schmidt, who was officiating the game and was a legend in Minnesota hockey, told me he had never seen that happen before and was sure that it had to be a record. I was the center for the team which means I was the one vying for the puck when it was dropped. I did the same thing twice in a row. When the puck was dropped, I knocked it between the other center's legs, got around him and went straight for the goal. I was fast enough to get past the defenseman before they could get to me. My shots on goal were in different corners each time. I often use the memory of that third goal when I need to pump myself up. When I think about it, I can feel the coldness of the ice, the sweat dripping from my helmet, and my mom and my stepdad, Lee, cheering from the stands as I looked at them and held up three fingers. My heart rate has elevated just retelling the story. It is a great feeling.

ACKNOWLEDGEMENTS

Thank you to my lovely wife, Barbara, for her proof reading and copy editing. Her loving encouragement and attention to detail and nuance helped make these stories come alive.

Thank you to my family and friends who put so much fun and joy into my life.

Thank you to all who helped me make sure of the accuracy of my stories.

Made in United States
Troutdale, OR
01/06/2024